IN THE WILDERNESS
WITH THE RED INDIANS

Bethany in the Wilderness

IN THE WILDERNESS WITH THE RED INDIANS

German Missionary to

THE MICHIGAN INDIANS

1847 - 1853

E. R. BAIERLEIN

(ca. 1893)

Translated by Anita Z. Boldt
Edited with an Introduction by Harold W. Moll
Foreword by Pastor Richard Latterner

 WAYNE STATE UNIVERSITY PRESS

GREAT LAKES BOOKS
A complete listing of the books in this series can be found at the back of this volume.

Philip P. Mason, Editor
Department of History, Wayne State University

Dr. Charles K. Hyde, Associate Editor
Department of History, Wayne State University

Originally published in German in 1888, 1889, and 1893 by Justus Naumann's Buchhandlung, Dresden.
Copyright © 1989, 1996 by Harold W. Moll, Midland, Michigan. Great Lakes Books edition published by Wayne State University Press, Detroit, Michigan 48201. All rights are reserved.

99 98 97 96   4 3 2 1

Library of Congress Cataloging-in-Publication Data

Baierlein, E. R. (Edward R.), 1819-1901.
[Im Urwalde. English]
In the wilderness with the Red Indians / by E.R. Baierlein; translated by Anita Z. Boldt; edited with an introduction by Harold W. Moll; foreword by Richard Latterner.
p. cm. — (Great Lakes books)
Translation of: Im Urwalde.
Includes bibliographical references.
ISBN 0-8143-2581-5 (pbk : alk. paper)
1. Baierlein, E. R. (Edward R.), 1819-1901. 2. Ojibwa Indians—Missions—Michigan—Saginaw River Valley. 3. Missionaries—Michigan—Saginaw River Valley—Biography. 4. Lutheran Church—Missions—Michigan—Saginaw River Valley. 5. Ojibwa Indians—Social life and customs. I. Moll, Harold W. II. Title. III. Series.
E99.C6B25313 1996   96-28165
266'.4177446'089975—dc20

TABLE OF CONTENTS

FOREWORD

Pastor Richard Latterner

The Great Lakes Chippewa (Ojibwa) tribe that Rev. Baierlein served as missionary is the same tribe that I serve today as missionary/pastor. I am an enrolled member of the Minnesota Chippewa (Ojibwa) tribe. Rev. Ottmar Cloeter, a colleague of Baierlein, was sent and trained by Loehe in 1849, and began work in northern Minnesota with my people.

Historical factors influenced the Indians' view of mission work prior to the arrival of German settlers. In 1659, fur traders had begun to invade the Great Lakes region. They were met with resistance by the Indian people. The Chippewa were very much aware that the Iroquois nation of the New York area had been destroyed and scattered by the French. Along with the fur traders came Jesuit missionaries, who attempted to protect the Indians from the traders. The presence of French trappers changed the way of life for the Great Lakes Chippewa. Chippewa hunters modified their traditional hunting practices with the availability of metal guns and knives. Men ceased hunting for immediate food needs alone. Soon Indian men not only engaged in the fur trade, they depended on it. Indian material culture and certain habits of life were radically altered. Then, as game grew scarce, hunters had to go farther and farther from their homes. Eventually the Chippewa began moving into Wisconsin and Minnesota in search of furs. This caused friction between the Chippewa and the Sioux, who had disliked each other before the land became an issue. But now the Chippewa had the advantage of European weapons.

In the Treaty of Paris of 1763, the French gave to Great Britain all the lands east of the Mississippi. Thus ended the relationship between the Chippewa and the French. The British took over where the French left off in the fur market and the relationship with the Indians. Along with the British came missionaries.

The Chippewa suffered serious economic dislocation following the years of the fur trade boom, though Indians were not the only ones unable to support themselves in the 1830s, as these were depression years for many settlers. Eventually the Chippewa began to sell land to the Bureau of Indian Affairs (BIA). Land cessions in 1837 and 1842 provided annuity payments to the Indians. The BIA did not intend to make the Indians dependent on annuity payments forever, and attempted to set them up as farmers.

The Chippewa people had seen sweeping changes prior to the invasion of the German settlers in the mid-1800s. Their whole economic system had changed dramatically and they could not go back to their traditional way of life. They saw the changes that had occurred with the incursion of the French and the British, and they saw that along with the fur traders and the BIA, missionaries also arrived on the scene. Now the Germans were coming. I am sure they felt that once more they would be exploited and once more sweeping changes would take place.

Despite this feeling toward the white settlers, Rev. Baierlein earned the trust and respect of the Indian people. He was then able to effectively proclaim the word of God to them. Baierlein was a missiologist with a firm understanding of the relationship of culture to the Gospel message. He understood that his role as missionary was not to impose his German culture on the Chippewa people. Baierlein allowed the message of salvation to transform the Bethany settlement into a

Christian culture that remained Chippewa in many other ways. He translated many Lutheran hymns as well as a forty-seven-page Catechism and a combination Bible reader and spelling book into the difficult Chippewa language. He respected the inherent leadership patterns of the tribe. When he encouraged the Indian people to make the transition from wigwams to log houses, he allowed the leaders to make this change first, and the others followed. Pastor Baierlein was a student of the worldview and way of life of the Indian people he served. His outstanding description of the spiritual worldview of the Chippewa people can be found in a chapter entitled "Religious Beliefs of the Chippewas" in Herman Zehnder's *Teach My People the Truth: The Story of Frankenmuth, Michigan.* Much of the belief system he describes is still current among Ojibwa people today.

Rev. Baierlein left Bethany in 1853 to do outreach work in India. The following year, 1854, was a significant one for the Great Lakes Chippewa. Reservations were formed, and the Indians were destined for a new way of life, reservation life. I wonder if Rev. Baierlein might have seen this change coming and if this played a part in his accepting his new calling.

Baierlein's fellow missionaries in Frankenmuth had a different approach to mission work among the Indian people. Baierlein sought to develop an indigenous church among the Chippewa. The Frankenmuth settlement, by contrast, focused on developing a German mission colony that kept German speech, dress, worship, and tradition. The Frankenmuth colonists were brave and dedicated servants of God. I wouldn't call them ethnocentric, but they had a nationalistic mind set that was common in their day. They feared that if they let go of their heritage, traditions, and language, they would lose their theological grounding, as well.

We cannot be too critical of the Frankenmuth colonists, since many missionaries today use a similar approach to Indian mission work. They tell the Indian people, in order to become a Christian, you have to be like us. You must worship on Sundays. You must use this hymnal. You must use this language and form. We see people across Lutheranism that feel that altering the historical, culturally laden liturgy will compromise the conservative theological foundation. I rejoice for those like Rev. Baierlein, who stood firm in doctrine but were bold in their approach to bringing the Gospel to others.

Pastor Richard Latterner is an enrolled member of the White Earth band of the Minnesota Chippewa Tribe. He serves as missionary at large to the White Earth and Leech Lake Reservations. A graduate of Concordia Theological Seminary, Ft. Wayne, he also serves as field counselor for American Indian ministries of Missouri Synod.

EDITOR'S INTRODUCTION

Harold W. Moll

In the Wilderness with the Red Indians is Edward Baierlein's account of his five and one-half years as a German Lutheran missionary in Michigan's Saginaw Valley nearly 150 years ago. In order to better understand the establishment of the colony of Frankenmuth, it is rewarding to look at the history of its founding. The colony members arrived in what is now known as Saginaw on July 10, 1845. A communal shelter was ready for occupancy at Frankenmuth on Saturday, August 16. The seventeen persons moved in on Monday, August 18, 1845.

The founding of the unique colony at Frankenmuth on the Cass River about fifteen miles from Saginaw was a sign of the times. Thousands of German Lutherans had migrated to the United Colonies to escape religious, political, and environmental persecution in Europe. The colony at Frankenmuth was founded for the purpose of bringing Christ to the native Michigan Indians. The protest movements of Martin Luther and other reformers continued the breakdown of the me-

E. R. Baierlein

dieval church's political power, culminating in France's Napoleon conquering the Papal See in 1798. Movements such as those of Livingston, Carey, Moffett, and others who carried the Gospel to natives in remote parts of the world are a matter of world history. The Millerite movement in the United States and Europe rose to its peak between the 1830s and October 22, 1844, the day they expected the second coming of Christ to this world. Moravian mission activity progressed rapidly and spread westward among the displaced Indians.

Also to be mentioned is the nine-year mission activity of John H. Pitezel and W. H. Brockway among the Superior Indians. What is unique about the Frankenmuth colony is that it was supported financially by the Mission Society in Germany to bring Christ to the Native Americans. Eventually it became part of the Missouri Synod of the Lutheran Church. It also supported mission activity in Minnesota and planned to set up a station in Oregon.

The idea for the Frankenmuth mission colony was that of Wilhelm Loehe, a Lutheran clergyman in Neundettelsaw, Germany. He had established a training school in Dresden for prospective missionaries to locate in India. The school was later moved to Leipzig so the students could get their secular training at the University of Leipzig. Loehe's attention was drawn to the needs of the Saginaw Valley, Michigan, in the United States by Lutheran clergymen in the Detroit-Pontiac area. Perhaps Loehe had read the 1831 reports of De Tocqueville, a Frenchman who wanted to go to the very limits of civilization. He chose the Saginaw Valley in Michigan. There he found a total of thirty persons, men, women, and children, young and old. This he described as the farthest boundary of civilization.

The Frankenmuth colony was formed in Germany and sailed as a group to the Saginaw area. The first building erected on the Cass River was a 30-foot-by-30-foot communal building, used for a residence, church and school. Pastor Craemer was persistent in his dedication to carrying the Gospel message to the Native Americans. However, he was hampered by bickering in the colony, and some of the members holding a constant grudge against him. In addition he was sick a great deal of the time with ague, probably malaria. Craemer appealed to Loehe for an assistant, and Edward Baierlein was sent to help him.

Edward von Vilseck was born of Catholic parents in Sierakowsky in Posen, Poland, on April 29, 1819. He was disinherited by his father and prohibited from using the family name when he joined the Lutheran Church in April 1841. He chose the name Baierlein, meaning Little Bavarian, which he retained the rest of his life. He was apparently reconciled with his family, since he married his cousin, whom he courted by mail. She arrived in Michigan from Posen, Poland, in February of 1848 and they were married the last of the month. Another indication of renewed family ties was that he later visited his parents and relatives in Poland, on his trip from Michigan to his new missionary post in India. Baierlein and family were received with open arms.

Baierlein began his missionary training in Dresden in October 1843, and graduated from the Leipzig school in 1847. He was scheduled to go to India after graduation, but sickness prevented him from leaving Germany. Upon recovery, and also as a result of the urgent call for a trained helper from Pastor Craemer, the twenty-eight-year-old Baierlein was sent to Frankenmuth, where he arrived June 11, 1847.

Baierlein and others soon realized that the "colony method" did not attract the Indians. To be successful the missionary needed to live with the Indians in their campsites. They needed to be taught English-not German as had been attempted.

Chief Bemassikeh[*] lived with his family tribe on the south side of the Chippewa River at Little Forks. The group was decimated by smallpox in 1837. The remnant then moved up the river. Bemassikeh, an intelligent and far-sighted man, saw that the primitive way of life of the Indians was doomed. He wanted his young people to learn sedentary skills such as farming, blacksmithing, cattle raising, and to have a knowledge of the three R's. On several occasions Bemassikeh invited Baierlein to come to his group, which had settled on 387 acres of land he had purchased along the Pine River. This was about seventy miles from Frankenmuth and about three miles north of present Saint Louis, Michigan.

Baierlein and wife responded to the chief's invitation and moved to Bethany (literally "the House of the Poor" because of the wretched living conditions there). The Indians built a new wigwam for them as a temporary shelter until a log cabin could be erected. The permanent building had one room for living quarters and an adjacent room that served as a church and school.

Baierlein and wife became actual members of the tribe. He was one of the few white men who learned to live with the Indians. He did this in order to demonstrate a Christian life and to bring them into a

---

[*]Bemassikeh was chief of the Bethany band of Indians. The German rendering is Pay-ma-se-kee, English rendering, Bamosey. Bemassikeh purchased land for his group in 1839 and 1842 three miles north of St. Louis, Michigan, which was later called Bethany. (See Appendix IV.)

Chief Bemassikeh addressing his men

Christian atmosphere. They shared the results of their hunts with the missionary and he shared all that he had with them. At each baptism, celebration of the ordinances, Christmas or other holiday, the Indians were welcomed into his home for a prepared celebration. Food was always provided for the occasion. The group became one happy family, sharing and sharing alike. The church membership grew.

Baierlein, because of his Christ-like actions, created a continual, loving atmosphere and was truly loved by the Bethany Indians.

In his five and one-half years of living and working with the Indians, Baierlein was able to induce them to clear the land of timber, to plant gardens and to build log cabins in which to live. Several of his pupils were able to secure jobs in the newly formed businesses in the area and later at the Mount Pleasant Indian Reservation. One of them, Philip Gruet, a grandson of Chief Bemassikeh, eventually assisted the government in transactions on the reservation.

Baierlein and his wife were dearly loved and trusted by the Bethany Indians. He was well respected by merchants, the nearest being forty-five miles away in the city of Saginaw. He shared his meals, food and relationships with the group in true Indian style. When he left Bethany the natives realized they were losing a true Christian friend and brother. The community was filled with sadness.

Because of Baierlein's administrative skills and his demonstrated ability to get along with the natives, and also because of a health problem that was aggravated by the Michigan weather, the German Missionary Society in Leipzig reassigned him to warm, sunny India, where he labored for more than thirty years. He returned to Europe in April 1886, and died at his retirement home in Clarems Montreux, France, on October 12, 1901, at the age of 82.

A note here to help the reader to better understand Baierlein's position with the Indians. When Miessler replaced Baierlein as missionary, he immediately labeled the Indians "Bread Christians." He no longer provided refreshments for the special church functions nor would he share supplies with them. When Baierlein left Bethany he was destitute and had to borrow money to pay his fare back to Germany. When the mission was finally closed, the Bethany Indians had ceased to confide in Miessler. In fact he could not find out whether the Indians of the Bethany group were going to claim land on the reservation. After the Bethany Indians had settled in the new reservation, the missionary moved to the Mount Pleasant area. Settlers were prohibited from living on the reservation. Miessler's home and mission headquarters were about ten miles from where his parishioners lived. Many of the group died. Food was scarce and the Indians were forced to go where hunting and gathering was available. The mission was forced to close.

IN THE WILDERNESS
WITH THE RED INDIANS

BY E. R. BAIERLEIN

Dedicated in True Love to My Beloved Life's Companion

Forty years have passed[*]
Since we joined hands.
Forty years of toil and labor,
Among the red and among the brown,
In the dark shadows of the wilderness.
You were motherly to the uncivilized
And they lovingly called you Mother!
These Red children are now home.
We pilgrims are still on earth,
Although our evening is drawing closer,
And our steps already falter.
Home above, we greet thee!
Open soon the golden portals!
We are strangers here on earth:
The red children there above,
Have waited for us, so long:
Home above, we greet thee!

Dresden 1888   E. R. B.

---

[*] It is difficult to translate the German poetry into English and retain the meter and rhyn
All the poems in this work, including this one, are literal translations.

CHAPTER 1

THE ORIENTATION

You who often wander
Through the landscape of green meadows,
Stand still at a deteriorating burial ground,
Rest a little to decipher
A half obliterated inscription
That was the work of poetic art,
Simple words, yet each a sign
Promising, yet inspiring horror and dismay,
Full of mighty inspiration
For the present and the yonder:
Stay, read the simple inscription
This nightmare of this uncertain remote world.

Do you love the mystery and beauties of nature?
Do you love sunshine on the meadow?
Do you love the shadows in the grove?
Rain showers and snow storms?
Mighty streams wildly rushing?
Down between pine palisades?
Do you love thunder in the mountains
That fall numberless,
As the flight of an eagle from his eyre?
Stay, read the simple inscription,
This nightmare of this uncertain world.

Far to the west, in the midst of five great lakes, in the United States of North America, is the state of Michigan, which extends into the lakes like a peninsula. This entire state was at one time a large virgin forest interspersed with a few prairies. When the wind blew over these prairies it resembled a beautiful wavy sea of grasses. Like a sea, it extended into the far horizon, where the waving green prairies and the blue of the heavens joined. A man on a horse would actually disappear in the grassy waves. The missionary decided to visit the red man in his wigwam. How happy and thankful the white foreigner was when he again safely had passed the swampy area with the sharp blades of grass and arrived at the familiar virgin forest.

Forty years ago, Michigan was still one great wilderness. Only here and there were small clearings to be found. Here human beings had selected to build their homes. Such a clearing was Saginaw, Michigan, in the middle of the state. The streets of the young city were marked on the trees, and were regularly laid out. Only here and there a house could be seen. There were two stores. They carried everything that people needed in this area, such as ironware, plows, and scythes, guns and gun powder, lead, window frames, tools to build homes, salt pork, wool and cotton material, tea, coffee, sugar, honey, wheat flour, cornmeal, boots, caps, bonnets, clothing, blankets, etc.

Money was not needed if one wished to purchase something. Everyone could bring his wares and trade for that which he desired: the farmer for his wheat; the Indian for his pelts. He who temporarily did not have anything to barter could receive what he needed, for the wilderness is honest. There was a post office north of the stores.

If one left Saginaw City, which was named after the Saginaw River, and rode in a northwesterly direction, he came to the Tittabawassee River.[*] As one traveled up the river for about twenty miles

---

[*]The main travel routes used by the Indians before the white man arrived were east and west. From the Muskegon River there was a short ford to the headwaters of either the Pine or Chippewa Rivers, then east on these rivers to the Tittabawassee River. From there they went either north to a ford to the Kawkalen River or south to the Saginaw River. From these rivers they went along the shore of the Saginaw Bay or Whitestone Point. Here occurred the great spring sturgeon run. The limestone along the shore around Whitestone point was the source of chert [flint] nodules, used in making knives, arrowheads, and spearheads.

The route from Saginaw used by the missionary was twenty miles northwest of Saginaw by the Tittabawassee River to the mouth of the Chippewa River. The Tittabawassee was forded. Then three miles west on the north side of the river to the

he passed a few single log houses with long distances between them, and then came to the Chippewa River, where both rivers join. If the river was forded, which could be done in summer when the water was low at the rapids, he came to a single log house, the last in this region. The friendly dwellers received travelers with a hearty welcome.

Here all paths ceased and unbroken wilderness followed. When one turned to the west, he soon had to ride across the Chippewa River and came to the Pine River. On the left side of the river a skilled eye could discern a path which often disappeared where the ground was hard or covered by fallen trees. No stranger could have found the way or would have dared to follow the path. But the red man was familiar and at home in his forest, like the citizen was in his home city.

One day, in the spring of 1848, two riders were on the trail soon after sunrise. One was a compactly built man* of dark red color in his late forties. He was a French-Indian who followed the red race like a shadow, and supplied the Indians with the needed hunting equipment and also at times with the destructive *ischkudawaba,* firewater. Now his black Canadian horse did not carry any wares. His rider had ceased to be a dealer and had become a guide and an interpreter for the mission. He spoke the Chippewa language, also called Ojibwa, and a passable English, though not without mistakes in his pronunciations. He could also speak some French.

His companion was in his late twenties, a tall figure and of pale face. He was a complete stranger in this wild area and still belonged to that group of rare men that left their fatherland, relatives, and friends to go to this far away land to proclaim the salvation of Jesus Christ our Lord and Savior to the poor Indian.

As soon as the riders had crossed the Chippewa River where the water reached up to the middle of their saddles, they found themselves in a fully unbroken wilderness. The solemn stillness which surrounded them made a deep impression on the stranger! He had imagined these virgin forests to be entirely different. He thought it would be like the German forests, only bigger and filled with wild animals. He found it

---

confluence of the Pine River with the Chippewa River. The Chippewa River was forded to the west side of the Pine River. The trail followed the south side of the Pine River for thirty miles west to the Bethany mission.

*James Gruet(t), son of a French trader of the Mackinac Island firm of Gruett and LaFramboise. The trader and his Indian wife had two sons, James and Peter, and a daughter.

entirely different here! Not a trace of wild rabbits, or the trusting doe, or the stately buck, that he saw as a boy in his homeland. The ride lasted ten long hours without the sight of a single animal, nor even the sound of a bird. Not that game did not abound, for hundreds of Indians lived from the hunt, but none appeared. The quiet and lonesomeness were appalling.

A rapid progress was not to be thought of. Even though the guide knew the way, he had to stop frequently because trees of different ages and sizes had fallen over the path. It was necessary to find a way around them without losing direction, which could happen very easily. The trees lay as great long corpses with extended arms. Uprooted trees with branches brought a lot of earth up with them. Some of these giants of the forest that had fallen and lay before them in every direction were already soft and rotting, already returning to earth from which they had sprouted. What a field of death and dying. Yes, the entire wilderness is such a burial ground. In awe the rider stands quiet and calm as the wilderness itself. Between these giants of the past lying round about, the future generation happily sprouts up. Many more in tender childhood are destined to an early death. The larger and stronger, which had reached youth and maturity, pushed the small and weak back and smothered them. Everything was entangled.

There was little progress possible for a man on foot, not to mention a rider. The guide drew his ax from his belt and cut a way through, so that the horses could leap over or creep under the branches. For many trees in falling had become entwined in other trees, so they did not reach the ground. When the riders were occupied in preparing a path, the horses could browse on the tender branches since these animals were accustomed to find their own food.

Farther and farther they went into this density where the heavens could be seen only at times when the sun stood high. No man met the lonely traveler, no game was frightened away, not even the call of a bird could be heard. Only the trees gave off weird sounds in falling, of old age, or of limbs rubbing together. Maple, beech, cedar, oak, ash, pine, fir, birch, ironwood, walnut, hickory, etc., stood among each other or in groups. Trees with needles were usually found in groups, not too close to each other and where the ground was harder.

Now it was necessary to ride through a one-and-a-half-mile-long swamp. Naturally there was no sign of a path, but here and there signs had been made on trees, which directed the guide to stay in the right direction. The horses sank up to the saddle in this marsh and worked hard to get through. It would have been inhuman to sit on them, but it was impossible to walk alongside of them without sinking into the marsh. The riders were compelled to dismount at times on a fallen tree, so the poor animals could rest a while and catch their breath. The slow progress gave the inhabitants of the swamp, the thousands of mosquitoes, the opportunity to attack the novice, namely the white stranger. He had to give up protecting his face. All he could do was save his eyes. Yes, the great solitude that had struck the stranger was now suddenly changed and he now complained about the ever greater company there! Even the horses bled around their necks and could hardly see out of their eyes.

After they had ridden through the swamp, horse with rider trotted off for a short stretch to make it possible to free themselves from the abundant enemies, while a great uninvited number still accompanied them. Now they came to an open place. The stranger looked around in astonishment. The guide said, "Once upon a time Indians lived here. Small pox killed them." How sad the open space appeared, which might have been pleasant in former days. Where were the graves of the red sons of the forest who lived here? How true was the sad plaint:

> Our fathers' graves carry
> No signs, no inscriptions.
> Who rests here, we'll never know.
> Only know they were our fathers.
> What origin or what race,
> Which old family tree?
> Where they came from is a secret.
> Only know they were our fathers.

The dust of their bodies mixed with the dust of the fallen trees and their ghosts go to their fathers' ghosts. Where? Is not God also the God of the heathen? Certainly, He is also the God of the heathen.

The Pine River flowed, in a large bend, close to the trail. Suddenly the interpreter sprang from his horse and hastened to the bank of the river. There stood three stones about two feet high of a peculiar form, like a sculptured bust, but not carved by human hands.[*] Upon the upper part, which represented the head, lay pieces of firmly pressed tobacco, the type that is chewed in America. The Indians had offered the tobacco to their *manitos,* spirits who lived, as they thought, in the stones. The shrewd French-Indian put the tobacco in his pocket, and said, "That comes in handy as my supply is low." Since 1853, one of these stones can be seen in the mission house in Leipzig.

For some time the sun could not be seen, even though it had not set, because the sun is only visible when it is high. For the riders it had disappeared and darkness in the forest increased. Suddenly they came to a large unusual clearing, where many trees were still standing, others had fallen. In between them they saw smoke from a destroyed bark hut which the members of Chief Bemassikeh's tribe were cleaning up. The wild barking of dogs announced their approach. They arrived in front of the chief's abode, and now were at the goal of their journey. What a poor, wild, hapless place it was. Only the most primitive people could live here.

What was it that drove these savage[**] people so far into this unapproachable forest, away from all civilized humans? Hunters they were, to be sure, and had to live in the woods. But where the forest is so immense is it necessary to go so deep into it? No, it is not. Like the wild game that these men hunt, they themselves are looked upon as animals and are hunted. That is why they live so far from the white conquerors of their land. For the Indians, it is only in the extreme far-off distance where they can find security. Those that stay close to the white man will soon be soaked up by civilization, as is the snow by the March sunshine. Oh bitter grief! that civilization and Christian people have to be such a stumbling block to the savages, against whom they rush, stumble, and dash to pieces. What powerful preachers are these forsaken burial grounds of the Indian for the descendants of the white conquerors and the deaf ears to whom they preach! Heartless, thankless, the plows will be pulled across them and their place will be known no more.

---

[*]See *Manito Stones Near Midland* by Harold W. Moll (1959). Manuscript copy in Grace A. Dow Memorial Library, Midland, Michigan.

[**]The terms *savage, halfbreed, children*, etc., as applied to the native American people must be recognized as a product of the mid-nineteenth century. Baierlein was already aware of the problem as this paragraph discusses.

The gray-haired chief stepped to the door of his hut to receive the guests. Quiet, sure, and dignified, he appeared. He looked with pleasure at the white stranger whom he had already met at Frankenmuth. The stranger looked deep into his eyes. He could only compare the black eyes of the chief with those of a deer. They were deep and without background, the same as the forest itself. No passion, no insincerity lay in those eyes; also no hope or pleasure of living.

Quietly and firmly the chief shook the hand of the stranger and invited him to enter his dwelling. This was a bark hut, only larger than the others. In the center was a fire on which the evening meal was being prepared. On both sides of the length of the hut were benches that rested on stakes in the ground. They were covered with tree bark the same as the hut. As there was no chimney, the smoke not only filled the hut, but also the eyes of the guests. Because of the fire, there was no place to stand, so they sat on the benches. These were also used as beds for the guests as well as the chief and his family. The rare guests were treated with venison and Indian corn, which was cooked in a large kettle that hung over the fire. This was to be the meal for the family and guests. As a special treat, the wife of the chief found some flour to make a dough. To bake it she laid it in the ashes of the fire. With considerable self-confidence she handed the half-burned, half-baked pastry to the guests. An old saying is, "Hunger is the best cook," and a ten-hour ride through the pathless wilderness is a perfect way to bring on an appetite. So this half-cooked pastry with the Indian corn easily went down the throat.

The conversation of the evening was about the plans for the next morning. A big council meeting was to take place. The meeting was to decide a very important matter for the entire tribe, important for the missionary and important for eternity.

The chief called his assistant, pointed to the heavens in the east and said, "Tomorrow when the sun stands there, I will expect the men here." The man hastened to deliver the message.

After a lengthy conversation they were ready to retire for the night. The saddles of the horses served as pillows and the hard bark benches served as beds until morning dawned.

About nine o'clock the men arrived. They were dressed in their best finery, which was rather odd to behold. Most of them wore trousers, which reached halfway up their legs to their hips and were tied at the top. On the sides they were embroidered with colorful beads. They wore soft deerskin shoes (moccasins). These were decorated with colorful beads and porcupine quills. A gay colorful stained shirt covered the upper parts of the body and dangled around their thighs. They threw a woolen blanket, like a toga, over the entire body. The raven black hair hung in a long braid down their backs. Eagle feathers adorned their bare heads, some had painted their copper-red faces with bright red stripes in order to show their festive mood. One grumbly oldster, who must have had a bad dream, had painted one side of his face entirely black.

The women also came. They wore similar shoes on their feet, and trousers; over this they wore a cloth or deerskin coat, richly embroidered with beads and ribbons, that reached halfway to the calves of their legs. The tops of their bodies were covered with short jackets and the busts were adorned with decorative beads and ornaments. The children ran around naked. Others that were not able to walk yet were carried on their mothers' backs wrapped in a woolen blanket.

After the men sat down on the logs that were lying around, the women squatted on the ground in groups. The chief then came to the door of his wigwam. Even he had dressed in his best for the occasion.

With his left hand he held his toga at his chest. He extended his uncovered right hand toward the group, and made a twenty-minute speech, which was well received, judging by the approving grunts. He closed with the customary *nindikit,* which means "I have spoken," upon which a long and loud *aouks* was uttered in response.

The interpreter gave a short resume of the speech. The chief had referred to the reduced circumstance of his race and said that he heard that his brother, this white stranger, had come to this land in order to help the red men and to show them the good and right way. As there was plenty of space in the area the chief had invited him to dwell in their midst. The stranger desired to meet all the men and talk with them. His coming or not coming to stay would depend on their decision. This is why he had called them together. Then he introduced his brother the *Mekadaekonjeh,* the Black Coat[*] who would also speak to them, etc.

---

[*]The Lutheran and Catholic missionaries to the Indians wore distinctive long, black coats. The Algonquin Indians referred to these ministers as Black Coat or Black Coats.

The Black Coat arose and spoke to the men. He spoke in English and in short sentences so the interpreter could repeat the message word for word. In order that the long journey should not be in vain, even if the men did not wish that he should remain with them, the missionary interpreted briefly the mysterious ways of God for their salvation and showed them the way to peace here and beyond. He indicated that under present circumstances he was inclined to accept the invitation of their chief and live among them. But there are two things he would ask of them and two things he wanted to do for them.

First, he wanted to show them the way to eternal life, that when they depart this world in death they would reach eternal bliss where there would be no pain, no sorrow, no hunger, no thirst, and no death. The second, that he wanted to instruct their children in reading, writing, and arithmetic. This was to enable their own children to read to them the good word of God and be prepared to keep their own accounts so they might know whether or how much they were being deceived by traders.

On the other hand, he would ask two things from them. First, that they would send their children to instructions and second, that they themselves would come every Sunday so he could teach them the ways of God. He asked them to consider this proposition.

A long silence followed. The men hung their heads as in deep thought. Then the chief asked, "Now what do you say?" Thereupon the oldest man, the one that had blackened the one side of his face, said, "We have nothing to say, we are waiting to hear what you say." The chief said, "As far as I am concerned, I will send my children to instructions and will appear on Sundays with my family to hear what the Black Coat has to say about the Great Spirit."

Another pause, then the men spoke one after another. Everyone that wanted to speak stood up, and closed their remarks with the *nindikit* after which a more or less *aouk* followed. The content of their speeches was about the same, that it would certainly be good to have the children instructed since none of them really knew how their accounts stood with the traders, and no one could read the paper upon which his debts were shown.

They all agreed to attend the Sunday meetings, if they were not too far away on the hunt. No one spoke against the proposition.

Since another pause ensued, the chief stood up again and made a sad, yet impressive speech. Many of the Indians are born speakers and know how to speak with propriety, tact, calmness, and fluency, without stopping or repeating or taking long to think about it. Every sentence is ready for printing. No matter how long he speaks, nobody interrupts, but waits for him to say what is on his mind and close with his *nindikit.*

Chief Bemassikeh was one of these orators. He looked into the far distance until he had something to say that concerned one or the other. We also looked into the far distance. He then quietly turned to those concerned. One could feel his eyes directly on us.

He took this opportunity to say that he was happy that the Black Coat had decided to remain among them. Then he said, "When I behold how low my race has sunk, it breaks my heart. There are many fires around us, but their warmth is not always good, for example, firewater and the houses of the trader. There are also many birds of our color that bring things here that are not good. If you go their ways and do as they do and carry on like they do, that would pain me very much. On the other hand, if all of you would be instructed in the manner our friend desires to instruct you and as I have observed in their church services in Detroit, I would be very happy.

"Especially you young women that have fallen by the wayside should make use of his coming to reform. Now I have little more to say. I consider the matter settled that he may come. I shall build the missionary a bark hut where he can live until he can erect a log house himself. I am an old man and my spirit will soon be with the spirits of my fathers. I wish that before I die that I will see my people enter a better way of life."

Thereupon he warned and admonished both men and women, as only a father could admonish his children. He walked toward the missionary and shook his hand heartily and long. This was a sign of friendship and acceptance into the tribe. The men stood up, one after-another, approached and shook the hand of the missionary so hard that his arm up to the shoulder hurt for days.

The married son of the chief said, "Being my father the chief calls you his brother, so I must and will call you my father and will respect you as my father." The other men agreed and "my father" became the name of the missionary in the wilderness from then on.

Thus the purpose of the trip across the ocean was attained. The white stranger became the guest and a member of the tribe. He was to live in the wilderness, a day and a half ride to the post office and a one day ride to the next human abode. His home now was in the midst of these wild heathens.

Gruet, the half-Indian guide, shook his head in doubt. But the missionary looked beyond the forest and beyond the clouds.

CHAPTER 2

THE LANGUAGE OF THE INDIANS

Stay on, traveler, hear the lamenting
Of a suppressed and subdued race.
Serious and simple are his words,
And your heart will be touched.

Pain and loathing you will feel
Against the white men
That oppress and crowd the red man,
Deprive and slaughter them.

Woe, the greed and earthly hunger
That clouds these weak brothers.
It is not right, this greed to follow,
It is only right, what God has ordered.

To prove that many Indians are born speakers, I will quote some of their speeches that deserve to be read. Soon this entire race will be forgotten, as you forget one that has died. These speeches will give us at least a glimpse into the heart of red man, a glimpse that will leave us with sad hearts.

To understand the situation under which these speeches were made, I will explain as follows. During the last war of the colonies with their English lords, the English commander of Detroit, Michigan, ordered the Indian chiefs to fight against the Americans. So the Indians were sent to fight on both sides, without any reason for themselves at all. They soon were aware of this. Above all, they had no intention of shedding the blood of the colonists for any reason. So the noble Chief Kakapan made the following speech to the commander.

"My Father! Some time ago you put this ax in my hand, and said, 'Try this ax on the heads of my enemies, the Kichemakoman (Long Knife), and let me know if it is sharp and good.' My Father, I had no reason or desire to war against this people that never were in my way. You say you are my father and I am your child, so I accepted the ax. Yet you withhold the necessary things that I need to live and protect myself with. I am not able to get any ammunition. Maybe you think that I am a fool, that I will obey your orders and put my life at stake. Above all, this is a problem that does not concern me at all, and I have nothing to gain. To fight against the Long Knife is your problem. You started this quarrel and it is up to you to settle it. You should not force the Indian, who you say are your children, and put them in danger for your sakes.

"My Father, it has cost many lives already, entire tribes have been thinned out. Children have lost their parents, wives their husbands, brothers their brothers, and who knows how many more lives will be taken before the brawl is ended. My Father, you probably take me for a fool and think that I would thoughtlessly attack your enemy. Do not think that I do not understand. As you know even at this time, though it seems that you will be enemies forever with the Long Knife, yet you must soon make peace with him.

"Mark my word, while you so persistently urge and goad us Indians on to fight your enemy and while I am rushing on to attack him with this deadly weapon in my hand that you gave me, what do I see when I suddenly turn and look back? I probably would see My Father clasping and squeezing the hands of the Long Knife. Yes, even those that he now calls his enemies. Then I would also see you laugh at my foolishness, while here and now I am risking my life by obeying your orders!

"Who among us could believe that you would love a race of different color more than you do the white, who are the same color as you. My Father, remember what I have said. Now here is the combat ax that you gave me. I have found out that it is sharp, as the scalp that hangs on it will testify. Even though I have not done all that I could have done, my heart failed me. I felt sorry for your enemy. I felt sorry for the innocent women and children who would have had to suffer, who had nothing to share in your quarrel. Therefore I did it differently. I spared his life. I captured someone. I took him alive. Then I got the idea to bring him to you. I caught sight of your little boats. I put the captive in the boat for you. You will receive him in a few days and you will find that his color is the same as yours. Do not destroy what I have spared. You have the means to save what I could have lost. The red warrior is poor, his hut is empty. But My Father, your house is always full"

The Indians were frequently required to assist in wars, whereby they always lost large stretches of land. Here is an example. Logan, a respected chief and friend of the Europeans, did not take part in the wars and also knew how to keep his people from taking part. It happened that some Americans decided to settle on the Ohio River where some Indians were living. The Americans carried on in such a cruel and inhuman way that the Indians could not have done worse. They gathered a great number of soldiers and then under Captain Cresap they followed the Indians. They soon caught a large number and shot them. On their way back they saw an old canoe with some women and children crossing the river. They shot them all. This happened to be the fine and innocent family of Chief Logan. Then Logan with a couple of other chiefs took up their weapons, but they were overcome and had to beg for mercy.

He then wrote the following words to the governor. "I ask you, did not every white man that came to Logan's wigwam and was hungry, was he was not given food? During the long bloody war, Logan quietly stayed in his wigwam, a friend of peace. My love for the white man was so great that my people referred to me and said, 'Logan is a friend of the white man!' But Cresap in cold blood murdered all my relatives, without any reason. Not one drop of my blood now flows in the veins of one living person. This now has called me to take revenge. I have hunted, I have killed many and have satisfied my revenge. I am happy for my country's sake, because of the signs of peace. But do not think that it is because of fear. Logan does not know fear. He will not flee to save his life. Who is left to mourn? No, not one!"

This short letter was admired, but Logan did not outlive it very long. He was murdered on his way home, as was another chief and his son, who tried to defend him.

After peace was declared, plans were again made to take more land from the Indians. A direct effort was made to have them take part in the war. At a council meeting which took place soon after between officers of the government and the Indians, Chief Makadawaniki (Black Thunder) stepped up and addressed the officers of the government.

"My Fathers, restrain yourselves, listen quietly to what I have to say. I will speak plainly. I do not speak with fear or trembling. I have never offended you and innocence knows no fear. I turn to all of you, red skin and white skin. Where is there a man who is my accuser? Let him step forward. My Father, I do not completely understand some of these transactions. Recently I was set free. Should I again be put in bondage? It is impossible for me to change my convictions. Maybe you do not know what I am speaking about, but it is the truth. Heaven and earth are my witnesses that I in every possible way have been forced to lift the war ax against you, but I would not! Because I could never believe that you are my enemy. If that is the behavior of an enemy, then I would never become your friend.

"You know that I led a secluded life at my former dwelling places. I called my warriors and we smoked the peace pipe and resolved to be a friend of the Long Knife. I sent you a peace pipe. It was like this one here. You received it. I told you that your friends should be my friends and your enemies should be my enemies. If that is the behavior of an enemy, then I could never become your friend.

"Why do I tell you this? Because it is the truth. It is a sad truth. The good actions and deeds are buried deep in the earth. Now the bad actions and deeds are undressed and stand naked in front of the world, so all eyes can see them.

"When I came here, I came in friendship. Little did I think that I came to make excuses. I have no more to say before this council, only to repeat what I already have said to my Great Father [the president of the United States]. It was simply this: My land could never be transferred or surrendered. Up to now, I have been cheated in every treaty. I have been shamefully and dishonorably defrauded. Again I will call upon heaven and earth to be my witness, and smoke this pipe, as a

36

sign of my sincerity. Are you sincere? You shall receive it from me. When it touches your lips, make the smoke soar upwards as a cloud and with it carry away all misunderstanding that stands between us."

Chief Metea spoke to the governor of Michigan in the following manner. "My Father, hear what we say in faith and good will. You know that at one time our land was very great and wide. Now it has shrunk to a little dot, and now you want that also. This caused us to do some serious thinking. You know we are your children. When you first came among us, we listened to you with open ears. As often as you asked a favor of us, our only answer was a willing 'Yes.' That you know yourself.

"Our fathers have all descended to their burial ground, they had common sense, but we are young and foolish. We do not wish to do anything that they would not approve of, if they were still living. We are afraid that we may offend their spirits if we sell this land that contains their burial grounds and we are afraid that we offend you if we do not sell it. This land was given to us by the Great Spirit, to hunt and grow corn on, to live and to die on. He would never forgive us if we sold it.

"When you first spoke to us about land in the north [Michigan] we said we had a little and agreed to sell you a piece of it. But you were immediately aware that we could not give away any more. You have never enough! We have already given away large stretches, but you are not satisfied. We have only a little left and that we need ourselves. We do not know how long we will live. We want our children to have a place to hunt. Soon you will take all our hunting reserve. Your children drive us ahead of themselves. We are beginning to worry. The land that we have traded to you you may keep. But we will trade you no more!

"You may think I speak violently but my heart has good feelings toward you. I speak to you as one speaks to his own children. I live on the land and hunt and I fish in the streams. My land is already small. How shall I feed my children if I give everything away? We have said everything to you that we have to say. This is what we have agreed upon at the council. What I have said is the voice of my people. We have no bad feelings. We speak to you with a warm heart and a good feeling of our friendship."

The hoary old Chief Black Eagle was captured in the war and was to be put in chains. Now, according to the Indian custom, he awaited a martyr's death. But he made the following speech before his enemies:

"You took me captive with my warriors. That pains me terribly. I had hoped, even though I could not defeat you, that I would be able to make trouble for you for a long time yet. I tried to get you by ambush. But your last general understands the Indians' war and ways. I decided to enter by force and fight you face to face, but your rifles aim well. The bullets flew through the air like birds and whistled around our ears as the wind in the winter whistles through the trees. My warriors fell around me. It was terrible. I saw my unlucky day before my eyes. In the morning, the sun came up gloomy. In the evening it set like a fiery bullet behind a black cloud.

"This was the last sun that shone on Black Eagle. His heart is dead. He is a captive of the white man. They will do with him whatever pleases them. He can endure the torture. He is not afraid to die. He is no coward. Black Eagle is an Indian. He did nothing that an Indian has to be ashamed of. He fought for his people, for his women and children against the white man, that came year in and year out to cheat and take our land away. You know the reason for this now. Every white man is familiar with it. You should be ashamed.

"The white man despised the Indians and drove them from their dwelling places. The Indians do not cheat. The white man speaks evil of the Indians and looks down on them with contempt. The Indian does not lie or steal. An Indian that would be as evil as the white man would not be allowed to live among his people. He would be killed and his body would be left for the wolves. We begged the white man to leave us in peace, but they followed us and trampled on our paths. They moved among us like snakes. They poisoned us by their movements. We were not safe anywhere. We became like them— hypocrites, liars, adulterers, lazy, gossips, and good for nothing.

"We went to our Great Father [the president of the United States]. His big meeting of council gave us nice words, big promises, but no help. Things became worse, there were no more deer in the forest, the marsupials [opossum] and the beaver fled. The source of our nourishment dried up and our women and children starved.

"We then looked up to the Great Spirit. We called a council meeting and lit a great fire. The spirit of our fathers stepped up into our midst. He advised us to take revenge of the wrong, or all die. We all spoke before the great council fire. It was warm and cozy. Our battle call resounded abroad and we took the battle ax in our hands. Our knives were ready. Black Eagle pounded heavily on his chest as he led his warriors into battle. He is satisfied. He will now go to the land of his spirits in peace. He has done his duty. His father will meet him there. He will praise him.

"Black Eagle is a real Indian. He will not mourn as a woman. He has a warm heart for his women, children, and friends, but is not concerned about himself. He is concerned about his people that will suffer. He bewails their destiny. Also, the white man does not scalp heads, he does worse. He poisons the heart. It is not safe to be in his neighborhood. The Indian will not be scalped, but in a few years he will be like the white man. You won't be able to trust the Indian anymore, you will need many officers among the people to keep a tight rein on them. For that is what the dwelling places of the white men are like.

"Farewell my people! Black Eagle tried to save you and revenge the wrong. He drank the blood of the white man. Now he is captured and his plans are ended. He can do no more. His sun has set and will not rise again. Farewell, my people!"

Treaties made with the Indians were effective for only a short while. The Indians were pushed further to the west. While war with them was shunned, the white man plotted to cause dissent among them in such a way as to win them by promises and illusions.

Under similar conditions the hoary Christian Chief Metoxen gave the following speech. "Brothers, I will speak to my red and white brothers for the last time. I am an old man, and soon my spirit will be with the spirits of my fathers. For many years I have stood at the head of my people. The white brothers pushed me from the state of New York. I said to my tribe, "Set up your wigwams here, you will find it a beautiful place." I had hoped to depart to my fathers in peace, from here. But now I see there is no peace. All treaties and transactions that have been made show that there is no peace for my people. I will enter my grave without any comfort.

"I wish to speak one more word to the Winnebago and Menominee. Brothers, it is not good that the white man has stepped among us. He keeps us apart. We used to live in peace with each other. We came here from where the sun rises [east] and begged you to give us a place to live. We said we had no home anymore at the burial grounds of our fathers, because the white man came. You took our hands and said, 'We are happy to see you. Here is our land and live among us.' We said, 'Give us a piece of land, that we can call our own, we will pay you.' You did this, and we made a solemn agreement. We were told that the white man would never come this far. The Great Father, the president of the United States, said, 'My white children shall never disturb you.' We lived together in peace till the white man came.

"Brothers, he has told you bad things and made you believe them. They were not true. He wants your land and not us! First he spoke sweet words to get on the good side of us, now that he has gotten power he says wild threatening words to us.

"Brothers, come back to us! We want to be one people [tribe] again. We want to unite and beg the Great Father, that he will take the white man back again. Upon my word the love and faithfulness of our tribe is not rusted, it is still clean and good.

"I will speak once more to my white brothers. Do not feel offended, because I have said the truth. You certainly saw it with your own eyes. It is all true that I have said to the Menominee and Winnebagos. We have told you of the promises that our Great Father the president made.

"Now you yourselves, our Great Father and his head officers, yes, you have to admit by testimony before the Great Spirit that what I have said is the truth.

"I am sorry, brothers, that it is not in your power, to let justice happen to us. We thank you for your good intentions. You say that your instructions do not allow you to make decisions on the existing matter. You offer us new agreements. First fulfill the old agreements! If we then need anything more, we will have grounds to trust your new agreements. Brothers, it is far better to have no agreement at all, than not to keep those that have already been made. We do not wish to be cheated again.

"My Brothers, we have learned something from the white man. That is, that we are able to trust the God of the white man. We believe that He is the one true God. The God of all mankind. We feel now, more than ever, we need to put our entire confidence in His care. The white man has done wrong to us and I do not know what new injustices my people can expect. Soon I will be going to my grave where the fathers of my father and the fathers of your fathers are, with the thoughts of the son of David which I read in the book [the Bible]. This book was presented to me by the king of England from the other side of the great sea.

"God is the witness of all our agreements or treaties. God was our witness when they took place. God will reward each according to his ways. My Brothers, I have spoken."

These few examples should suffice and show the gift of speaking these Indians have. But they make a greater, far greater, impression when you hear and see them speaking in person. Their actions, grace and tone of voice is so natural and complete, as if they had practiced for a long time and had good teachers.

Yes, God will reward each according to his works, namely, praise and glory and immortal life to those who in patience and good works strive for eternal life. But those who are quarrelsome and do not hear the truth and only listen to the unrighteous, and live a life of disgrace and hatred that destroys the souls of man, they will go to hell.

Praise, honor and peace to all that do good. God is no respecter of persons. How much distress and anxiety man could spare himself if he would leave evil and would only do good.

We must not keep the truths of God from the Indians. They are to be pitied. Earth does not satisfy hunger and wealth does not satisfy thirst. Only the Bread of Life, that comes from heaven, gives the world life and stills the hunger of the soul. Only he that drinks the water of life will never thirst

"Blessed are those that hunger and thirst for righteousness, for they will be satisfied."

CHAPTER 3

THE WIGWAM OF THE INDIAN

Also, in a wigwam of the Indian
If the Lord is there with you.
If He is absent, nothing is secure,
Even if it be a king's castle.

Only go where he calls you,
Do what he dictates.
Do not be afraid. In His presence,
Death itself is your gain.

Then live the life you live
In Him alone, only in Him
Resurrection and life.
In Christ alone, for you and me.

The Indians call their dwelling place a wigwam. These are made of trees and tree bark. The bark is peeled off the trees in four-foot strips and as wide as they can get it. When bark dries it rolls together, so it has to be laid flat on the ground and weighted down with stones or heavy wood, till it is dry and stays flat. This prepared bark serves as the walls and roof of the wigwam. If it is only a temporary hunting hut, two rows of bark are set up and tied together. For a regular home, two rows of bark are tied to the poles that are stuck in the ground. They are tied with dried grass or thin roots. The walls are about four feet high. Then the roof is put on. The roof bark is also tied to the poles. In the center top a two-hand-wide opening is left for the smoke to escape. Both ends and the gable are also formed from tree bark. In one end a small opening is left that serves as the entrance. A curtain is hung in place of a door. The curtain often is an old torn wool blanket.

When the exterior of the wigwam is finished, the interior of the better homes have benches added. They are about one and a half feet high, resting on poles that have been pounded into the floor. The benches are on both sides, along the length of the wigwam. They are covered with tree bark. You sit, eat, and sleep on these benches. Because of the damp floor, these benches are a benefit. Of course, they are hard, a lot harder and more uneven than the floors.

Chief Bemassikeh, as promised, assigned a wigwam as a temporary home for the Black Coat when he arrived with his luggage. It was very nice inside. After a long journey it was very comfortable to rest upon a wooden bench, the fire at his feet, and be able to gaze beyond the stars. It was also very pleasant to be alone and not always in the midst of the Indians, who observed every movement and every gesture. Yes, for the first night it was very pleasant. But on the next day it was found that not everything in the wilderness is perfect. The missionary had not learned to sit with crossed legs, so he sat on the bench with his legs on the ground. This did not work because of the fire in the middle. And how was he to write? This was a must, in order to learn the difficult language. He tied a couple of pieces of tree bark to a couple of stakes for a table. It really was a sad looking table, but then there was no room for the fire. So the fire was moved outside by the door. When it rained the fire would not burn. The rain also found the opening in the roof that was intended for the smoke. It was not clean rain from the clouds anymore. It had washed the black smoke from the bark and came down the color of ink. It filled the cups and plates on the bark table. He often had to hold an umbrella in one hand, while he used the other to hold the spoon. But it worked.

At night the rain came in from above and the sides. Even though the umbrella protected the head, the rest of his body, his books, and everything else, were soaked. Hence the longing for a log house with a solid roof became even stronger. Soon the plans were made, but here, so far from all human help, this was no easy project. Of course, the Indians do not work! More about this later.

Because the fire was not kept inside the wigwam the numerous dogs of the Indians found their way into the wigwam. Dogs instinctively keep away from fire so as not to burn their feet. During the day the chance for a meal escaped them because of the missionary inside the dwelling. But at night they found their way inside. Now there was no more sleep for the missionary. He had to change and fortify the entrance to the wigwam with pieces of tree bark, so the dogs could not enter by the door. They then went up on the roof of the wigwam and looked down from above. The leap into the wigwam seemed to be too risky. They then raised a weird howling on the roof. They would not listen to reason and when chased away, soon returned. Finally, they chanced the leap to the inside and greedily devoured whatever they found. This of course was not much. Sometime later the wife of the missionary arrived and lived in the wigwam. The dogs continued to bother it. They ate one and a half pounds of "light" which the efficient housewife had made from venison tallow for candles. The dogs also broke many a cup and saucer. But then, luxuries do not rightfully belong in a wigwam!

Even though it was not a permanent home, it often was a welcome shelter for the missionary. After a ten- to twelve-hour ride, both horse and rider arrived exhausted and hungry at the wigwam. The Indians were always friendly and willingly shared what they had. Often there was not much at hand. They always seemed to have a piece of dried venison or bear meat and gladly shared it with the white guest.

One day the missionary visited a distant Indian group. Several visitors had come to the wigwam to hear the missionary. Meal time came. The family had a limited food supply, but as is the Indian custom, what they had was willingly shared with all. Dried meat and corn were cooked together. The kettle was lifted from the fires and set down in the center of the circle of men, which included the missionary. A large wooden spoon with a hook on the end was hung from the kettle. One person took the spoon and filled his mouth three or four times. He then handed the spoon to the next man, who did the same. When the missionary's turn came, he tried to do the same, but he was not accustomed to such a large spoon, so lost most of the food by spilling it down each side of his mouth. This would have been funny if the hungry men had not been waiting for the spoon. He quickly had to get as much as he could and then pass the spoon on to the next man.

So it went till the kettle was empty and that did not take very long! For when hunger demands its rights, eating is thoroughly in earnest. The missionary was hardly aware that there was not a grain of salt in the entire kettle. The Indians live without salt though they use it when they have it. That is seldom and they do not miss it. It is remarkable how a person's appetite forgets salt and lard.

During the meal, very few words were spoken. But when this important process was over the men relaxed with their feet toward the center and the conversation began. The missionary sought to present his message as much as possible and then tried to learn the views of the Indians.

Where no literature of the people exists, their views can best be obtained from their legends remembered by the older people. It does not matter how much or how little these legends are true, they are still very important because they express the lore of the people. The Indians have many legends, which are told in widely different versions. Most of these wigwam legends are about the origin of sin, the creation of man, and the question, what will confront man after death?

The Indians believe that the world is filled with spirits, which the Chippewas call *manitos*. The *manitos* live in mountains, trees, stones, in lakes, waterfalls and hurricanes, etc., and are able to take on the form of humans and animals. Most of these *manitos* are neither good nor evil, but powerful to help or to harm. Also the winds are *manitos*. Among them is especially Kiwedin, the north wind. It is to be feared since it causes so much suffering in the winter. The Indians count their birthdays according to how many winters they have survived.

Over all the *manitos* is the Kitschimanito, the Great spirit God. He especially favors the red man, but for some reason or other has neglected him for a long time without bothering himself with the fact that things are not going well with the red man.

The wigwam legend of the origin of the bad creatures is told as follows: Metowack, which people now call Long Island, was a great primitive tract of land that looked as if the sea had suddenly receded and left the sandy ground dry as a mud cake on a flat platter, then layered on the sea. This was Metowack.

Here is where Kitschimanito decided to settle, and here he could create new creatures. Here he not only had enough room, but also was not disturbed, since the sea encircles the spot. Some of his experiments were so mammoth that they were hard to control. Kitschimanito gave these creatures suitable strength, so they could apply it as they willed. Then when it pleased him he took the granted life back. He cared for these great creatures and set them up as experiments. If they misused their strength, he took the life from them again, before they could leave Metowack. If they pleased him, he would allow them to leave. This they usually did. On the northern end of the island they would plunge into the sea, then swim to the opposite forest and disappear.

Once Kitschimanito worked on a creature so mammoth that it appeared like a mountain on the island. All the spirits came by to see what it would be. The *nibimaber* [water spirits] looked up out of the sea. The *puckwadjinis* [dwarfs] were full of mischief and crawled in and out of the eyes and ears of this lifeless manito with the thought that Kitschimanito would not see them. But he saw them. He can look through anything. He was pleased with their liveliness. He was always thinking of new forms to create.

Now that this great monstrous thing was finished, Kitschimanito was afraid to give it life. So it stayed on his worktable, Metowack. Because of its great weight it finally sank into the ground. But the head and tail did not fully disappear. Then Kitschimanito opened its back and found a great convenient hole in which he could throw all the other creatures if they did not make the test. In this way a great mass of curious figures gathered in the belly of the animal.

Kitschimanito once created the evil one. He took two pieces of clay and formed two large panther feet. Then he stepped into them and walked around. He found them light and comfortable. He also discovered one could move around quickly without making noise. He added two legs like his own to the panther feet and let them walk around. This pleased him so he added a belly with long scales, like an alligator's. A long black snake happened along. Kitschimanito grabbed it and attached it to the body. It made a fine long tail. He made shoulders wide and strong like a buffalo ox, all covered with hair. The neck was short and thick.

As Kitschimanito worked on this new creature he did not give it much thought. But before he made the head he thought and studied a long time. He took a round piece of clay and worked on it with great care. He made eyes like a crawfish's, that could look in any direction.

47

He made the forehead high. Here was to be the brain that would have the subtlety of a snake.

Suddenly Kitschimanito stepped back and observed his new creation. He had only two feet, stood upright, and could see all things. He finished the head with strong jaws, wide lips, ivory teeth, and a nose like a vulture's. He set the quills of a porcupine on the head for hair. He set the head on the trunk. This was the first upright walking creature he had ever made. It gave him the idea of making man.

Night came. Bats flew through the air. A great storm raged over the island. All the animals began to howl. A panther came by and stood with raised claws before the figure. He smelled the feet that were similar to his. A vulture soared down and would have grabbed the nose that was similar, but Kitschimanito covered the creature's face to protect it. The storm raged. Each creature of earth was attracted to that part of the creature that was like him.

Many days and nights passed, yes, entire years passed by. Kitschimanito raised his head to the stars and meditated. A bat sat down on the creature's head. He grabbed it, took off its wings, and made ears for his creature. Kitschimanito saw that it needed arms and hands. He made them like his own. Kitschimanito was not happy with the figure. He was almost sorry that he had finished the figure. He put fire into it. But fire is not life. Fire burned the clay from which it was built. The fire glowed through the scales of the chest, the crawfish eyes glared like live charcoal. It had a fiery appearance.

Kitschimanito looked into the side of his creature. He decided to give it a little life, but did not remove the fire. The figure was very ugly, but sometimes it would smile viciously at Kitschimanito. After giving it much thought, he decided it was not good to let a creature like that live because it was made from parts of other creatures. It was gifted with arms and great strength. It had a chin and was able to hold up its head. It had lips and could close its mouth and lock its thoughts inside itself. While thus thinking, he grabbed the creature and tossed it into a cave.

But Kitschimanito forgot to take back its life. The creature was now lying unconscious in the bottom of the cave because of the great fall. He lay in the midst of the animals which Kitschimanito had thrown in the cave without life.

The Lord of the living though for a long time. The idea came to him to create a figure with two legs, arms and hands, made in his own image. This creature could then make bodies in the world using the spirits of the world.

After some time Kitschimanito heard a great uproar in the cave. He looked in and saw the monster sitting up and the good for nothing animals that had been discarded were gathered around him. He had given them life.

Kitschimanito took a great heap of earth and stones and stuffed the entrance to the cave and then left. Soon there was a great uproar inside. The earth rumbled. A thick vapor-like smoke ascended from the ground. The manitos [spirits] gathered at Metowack to see what was happening. Kitschimanito also came. He remembered that he had forgotten to take back the life when he threw the monster into the cave.

Suddenly a great mass of stones and earth was raised. The heavens were concealed by darkness. Storms raged. Flames shot out of the earth toward the sky and water was thrown high in the air. All manitos fled for fear as the horrible raging monster stepped from the cave. His life took on strength. The fire inflamed it. All that had life fled from him. They screamed, "Kitschimanito! Kitschimanito! You have made the bad spirit, the devil."

These are the legends of the formation of the bad one.

Kitschimanito is still thought of as powerful but not almighty. He is also wise, but not omniscient. At times he seems kind and friendly. All beings are descended from him. According to his thoughts, he created two different creatures and he gave them life. He could also take life from them. Childlike and childish, as the saying goes, they are really not bad. The bad is in oneself. It is not Kitschimanito's will in the world, but almost unintentional. Ask the Indians if they believe these sayings, they usually say they do not know, that is the way they heard them, but if they really happened, they could not say, because it was so very, very long ago.

The language of the Indians is so rich and refined that it seems as if it had been made up by philosophers. There is however something of this philosophic sense in the legend of the origin of evil. Evil did not come from itself. If it had, then there would be dualism, a doctrine that the universe is under the dominion of two opposing principles, one of which is good, the other evil, as the Persians believe. It also did not come from the will and design of God. He only gave life to good creations. So, in a sly, roundabout way they laid the blame on the forgetfulness of Kitschimanito. Man can only think of God as being much mightier and wiser than man and that mistakes and forgetfulness are natural. Only on the day of manifestation will man rightly understand it all. That is when God himself will reveal all His works and ways. Without this revelation all mankind, even the well educated, fumble around in the darkness, without really knowing God.

As the apostle John said, "The heathen do not know anything about God." And these heathen at that time were not Hottentots, a people of South Africa apparently akin to both the Bushmen and the Bantus, but were refined and educated Greeks and Romans.

Now the legend among the Indians of the creation of man follows.

Kitschimanito stood on a high hill and looked down on his creation. What a difference there was between him and other beings. He wanted to bridge over this difference and create beings which were between animals and manitos. Therefore he selected fine dust from the earth and formed a figure with his hands. He blew on it. There stood a white man before him. He looked pale and sickly. The great spirit was disturbed. He spoke to the white man and said, "You are really not what I desired, still I will permit you to live, step aside!" Once more he took dust from the earth and blew on it. There stood the red man. He smiled happily at the red man and nodded to him. That was what he wanted.

Kitschimanito spoke, "Come hither my children. White man you are not my favorite, but because I gave you life first, you shall be superior. Here are three boxes which decide your life. Choose which you want." The white man looked carefully into all three boxes before he decided. He exclaimed, "I choose this!" It was full of paper and books, quills [pens] were there and everything that is needed in the making of books. "Take them and use them correctly," said Kitschimanito. Then he called the red man and said to him, "Come here my favorite and choose." The red man looked only in the box that was before him. These were bow and arrow, war clubs and hunting knives. "I choose these," he exclaimed without looking back. "Take them my favorite and use them correctly." Finally Kitschimanito spoke to the black man, "Come here and take this." It was a box of hoes and axes and other equipment the black man needed when he worked for the white man and the red man.

Therefore the red man could not doubt that he was the favorite of Kitschimanito. His manner of life pleased the creator and he was to roam in the forest as the wild animals. This was the Indian's joy of life, and this was also what Kitschimanito expected of him.

But the Indian noticed that something was not right. It seemed Kitschimanito had withdrawn himself and paid no attention to them and did not care for his favorites any more. Therefore they came into the hands of the manitos. The Indians hardly ever mention the manitos, for they have an intense fear of them. They enjoy talking about Kitschimanito. They had a depressing feeling that at one time the Indian enjoyed a better standard of life and association with God, which by their own fault had been lost. Since they cannot find their way to Kitschimanito they try to serve the manitos, and have to satisfy themselves with them.

In case of sickness the witch doctor is sought, who pretends to represent the manitos and to determine the root of all illness as well as its cause and cure.

Chief Bemassikeh suffered from tuberculosis and wished to be well again. The missionary could only relieve him, but could not promise a cure. The chief sent for a noted witch doctor. He came and built himself a good barrel-shaped hut, made of stakes and the inner bark of trees. He then jumped from the top into the hut, and then he began his magic, accompanied by drums and clappers. With a mighty far-reaching voice, he chanted his exorcist formula. After a lengthy song, he suddenly became silent. "What is wrong?" said the sick chief, who lay nearby. "The manitos do not want to come," answered the witch doctor. "Why not?" asked the chief. The doctor said, "They say the white man is too near." By that, he meant the missionary [Baierlein]. The missionary had heard the weird chant during the night, but did not know its meaning. The chief wanted to help the situation and asked the doctor to move to a different place in the forest. They moved about twenty miles from the missionary's home. The witch doctor, chief Bemassikeh and several of his men assembled at that place. After the usual preparation, the loud chanting songs echoed far into the woods all night.

It happened that at this time the missionary was returning from a trip and was still traveling, although it was after dark. As he approached the place he heard the loud chanting on the other side of the river. He knew that no Indians lived there so he was curious to know what was going on. He got off his horse and tied it to a tree. He found a canoe, that is, a hollowed tree trunk, on the shore. He pushed it into the water, stepped into it, and paddled toward the singing. He intended to surprise them. But the dogs discovered him and started to bark. Immediately the singing stopped.

When the missionary stepped on the bank of the river he saw a number of figures lying on the ground completely covered with blankets. Like mummies they lay there without moving. He walked past them. No one moved. At the fire sat the witch doctor, who with a bold and brazen face just stared at him, without saying a word. The missionary noticed that something was wrong. What it was, he did not know.

Since his presence evidently was not desired, he went back to the canoe, crossed the river, and with his horse rode on into the night. Finally, he lay down under a tree and awaited the dawn.

Sometime later, the son of Chief Bemassikeh, who had become a Christian, explained to the missionary the meaning of the entire affair. His appearance, as the witch doctor said, had hindered the arrival of the manitos, who shuddered to be near the poor white man.

The Indians live a life of utmost freedom. They set up their huts or wigwams wherever they care to. They fell as many trees as they like, hunt any game that is at hand and for a change enjoy fishing. In the spring there is great rejoicing because thousands of three-or four-foot sturgeons come up from Lake Huron and spawn in the rivers. They are caught with long two-pronged spears. Everybody is happy. Sometimes when a sturgeon is impaled on the spear that is held by the Indian, it pulls the canoe and passes the other canoes. This makes the Indians especially happy. The catch is unusually precious. The meat is served dried and smoked. The caviar lies around in heaps and nobody pays any attention to it. At this time you live on fish and that without salt or lard.

In the spring it is fishing, in the fall it is the hunt that keeps them supplied with food. There are plenty of deer and fat bear. There are happy feasts. The women open their treasures of goodies they have raised and bring their share to the feast. This is corn, that they planted and harvested.

Raising corn is not such a difficult job and is considered a task of honor. The men have to furnish the game and fish the year around, so the women take care of the corn and sugar.

Corn is planted in the ground without preparing the soil. Four kernels of Indian corn are put in the ground one step apart and then covered with earth. The tree trunks and stumps that stand and lay around do not keep the corn from growing.

As the plant shoots up, a little more earth is added around the growing plant. This they do till harvest time. In good ground the plant grows quickly, sometimes six to eight feet and higher. Long ears with twelve to sixteen rows of corn grow on the stem. It has pretty gold and colorful kernels. It is a beautiful crop, and multiplies up to sixty, eighty, and even up to a hundred times. Harvesting corn is a time of real rejoicing and the women feel more important at this time than they do at any other time of the year.

Sugar-making is also a happy time. Usually by this time the corn has been consumed and the hunt, at this time of the year, is not very successful. Often Indians then live on sugar alone. Sugar does not take much effort to produce. The women scatter in the forest and look for areas where maple trees are plentiful. These are then tapped with an ax. They make a wedge or spigot of rolled up birch bark and insert it into the tree so that the sap runs freely into the vessel which is placed underneath. When the vessel is full, it is emptied into a kettle that hangs over the fire and the sap is boiled down. The sap has a tendency to boil over, so a woman takes a pine twig and beats the boiling sap, which causes the foam to recede. At the right time the kettle is taken from the fire. The thick sap is stirred for a long time till it turns into good, sweet brown sugar. This then is packed into twenty- to thirty-pound nicely decorated boxes made of birch bark. It is often sold to dealers. Sometimes the women make really pretty little figures of this sugar, such as a tortoise shell, and other forms. This is usually given to visitors as a gift. But out of necessity the sugar is usually eaten.

One time the missionary was on a trip and had had nothing to eat for three days but maple sugar. Soon his stomach burned so badly that he could not sit on his horse anymore. A woman was so moved by pity for him that she took the last corn soup she had from her children's mouths and handed it to the missionary. Though forty years have passed, to this day he has never forgotten this good deed of compassion.

Altogether the Indians seem to have a happy life, but have they? Now, according to the wisdom of the Castle of Laziness of our socialists, anarchists, communists, nihilists, etc., with their preconceived ideas, one has to go through blood and horror in hopes to accomplish happiness here.

The Indians have had all this free and without paying for a long, long time. The Indians do not work and do not pay any house rent. They do not have any police officers and no military. They also have no forced attendance at school or any other restraints. They live as free as the deer they hunt. The present expensive pleasure of hunting that we have on the Continent, they have had free every day of the year and for a change an abundant catch of fish. Now, are they blessed? Yes, when freedom from work and abundance of food are a blessing. But by comparison, fatted swine would be the most blessed group on earth.

But man, the thinking man, carries his blessings, as well as his misfortunes, around with him in his heart. If he lives in the wilderness, in a wigwam or in a place surrounded by blooming meadows, that would not affect his blessings or his misfortunes. If man stands in harmony with God, who created him, something like a breeze surrounds him, and he cannot escape from it, whether in life or death or even after death. In God, then, man has found the point of his origin, namely the Father. The only way to come to the Father is through Jesus Christ. He is then, through Jesus Christ, in good standing with God. Then he has found rest for his soul and peace in his heart. Then the life in the wilderness and in the wigwam is blessed. For he that gives himself to the Father becomes His child. He will be near them, and will feed their life and soul and protect them from all harm and danger. He that cares, protects, and watches over us has all this in His power.

These are not theories, for he that gives this testimony has experienced it. And after years of retirement from the wilderness, the wigwam, and the log house, he still looks back today, in his old age, to these years of joy, peace and blessings.

To live in this world without God is unfortunate for mankind. No matter what the color of his skin, white or red, to be in disharmony and conflict with the supreme beings is unfortunate. God is so powerful and is near to us everywhere. Without him we cannot live. From Him we can find nowhere to escape. To be without God is a misfortune of mankind. For such a situation does not let the soul rest or give the heart peace. There is always worry and fear and the entire life is without any goal or meaning. When deep in the wilderness or in suffering, without God there is no comfort, and in death there is no hope.

You may ask about the situation of the Indian. I would say the same as Old Sirach said. He said it very well and exact, as if he had lived among them. Indeed he says it with mighty powerful words:

"It is a miserable and distressing thing that all men's lives, from coming out of their mother's womb until the day of their burial into the mother of all, that their thoughts and fears of the heart, their imagination of things to come and the day of their end are labor to them. It is so for him that sitteth on a glorious throne, unto him that is humbled in earth and ashes; from him that weareth purple and beareth a crown, to him that is covered with rough linen. Wrath, envy, trouble, unquietness and fear of death, continual anger and strife, the sword, oppression, famine and affliction, and scourges are his. All these things are created for the wicked and for their sakes came the flood."

CHAPTER 4

IN THE LOG HOUSE

Now the wigwam is abandoned,
That old smoked up wigwam.
Now a log house, stands there, finished
With three windows, and two doors!
What a building in this wilderness,
Who would have ever thought of?
Yes, the white man is strong and mighty.
He is a mushkikiwinini,
He is a magician great and mighty.

Even though the wilderness is large, the dwelling places are very small. A large log house, twenty to thirty feet long, was planned. Fir trees were cut, and the logs were trimmed and hewn. The logs were grooved at the ends so they could be fitted at right angles at the corners. The foundation was usually made of large oak logs.

Several friendly German men came seventy miles from the colony of Frankenmuth to help the missionary build the log cabin.

The roof was made of shingles [shakes] that were cut and split. Two doors and three windows were placed and installed. A fireplace and chimney was built at one end of the large room. After caulking between the logs of the building was done, it was finished. The inside was divided into two rooms as usual. The small room served as study and bedroom. The larger room, about eighteen feet square, was the all-in-one room. Here the cooking and baking was done. It was the storage and dining room, living and visiting room. School was held here during the week. Also church services took place on Sunday. There were many native visitors. They were astonished to see a log house standing in this wilderness. They were especially interested in the fireplace. The fire burned so brightly and no smoke came into the house, or in the eyes, as in the wigwam, but all went up the chimney. The first thing the men did when they came in was to go to the fireplace and then look up the chimney.

Chief Bemassikeh came every day. He sat and listened to the instructions and sometimes took part in the conversation. In summer, when it was hot, he wore only a brightly colored shirt, while his legs were bare up to his thighs.

When classes started, the parents who had promised to send their children were notified. About fifteen or twenty boys and girls came. Since there were no benches or tables, they had to sit on boxes and trunks or on the floor. It was difficult to keep them quiet and together. It just could not be done, so the missionary and his interpreter split logs and made some really heavy, awkward benches. They also needed a table. A linden tree was split in three parts and fitted together. This made a strong but not very even table-top. Instead of legs, two Andrew crosses or saw horses were made and the table-top laid on it. You could write on it or even eat from it.

Because some of the children were entirely turned over to the missionary, he soon became the family father. Through the entire week, it was a lively place. Even more so on Sundays, as this was also the room in which church services took place.

The services here were entirely different from the ritual they were used to in Germany. Young and old, big and small, sat among each other, around the missionary, on benches or on the floor. The boys were unruly, the children played and yelled, while the mothers yelled just as loud, trying to quiet the children. One neighbor would chatter with another, loud enough to interfere with the sermon. That would cause the ears of the listener to turn to them, instead of the missionary. An old gray-haired Indian, maybe with his face painted black, lit his pipe with steel and stone. Now, while he relaxed and smoked his pipe, another raised his voice and asked for a fire. Another got up and joined the smokers. The men started to talk amongst themselves. The children started to walk around and leave. Thus it went on through the entire service. After a firm warning that it was necessary for their peace of soul to listen to the word of God, they became more quiet, and the missionary had hopes again. Then an Indian stood up and extended his hand, showing that he wanted to express his understanding of peace. He said that he did not hate the missionary, because he lived among them, but would not follow his advice. When the missionary asked if they understood him, one answered, "Oh, yes I understand it. This is not the first time that I have heard it." Another one asked, "What do these things have to do with the zodiacal lights?" These kinds of situations certainly are not very inspiring, and do not make preaching in a strange language, assisted by an interpreter, very easy. On the other hand, "The word of promise is that it shall not return empty." That is consolation enough not to get discouraged. At least they were still coming to the services.

Such were the beginnings in the wilderness.

Winter came and with it much suffering. The autumn rides the missionary took in this severe climate, often overnight, riding through swollen icy streams, without being able to change into dry clothes later, put him down in a bed of suffering. One time it happened along the way, fifty miles from home. He was detained there for fourteen days before he could finally start for home. When he arrived, he was greeted with the news that the Indians planned to kill him for his labor of love. There are few problems with the sober Indians, but the drunk and those that are stirred up are feared. Here he was surrounded by people whose hands were already stained with blood. Yet this had no influence on him, except that he often thought of leaving. But he had committed his life to helping in the mission field before he left Germany.

The above-mentioned illness that happened so far from his wilderness home was a serious situation. It was late autumn and the rivers were rising. Frost came, so that drifts of ice were forming. He had to hurry to get across the river, but could hardly move, as he was so plagued with fever and asthma.

He thought of tying himself between two horses, as the Thorstensons inadvisably did during the Thirty Years War, but then there would not be enough room for two horses to go side by side on the trail. He had to confine myself in the cabin of a friend. Pastor

Sievers of Frankenlust was informed of his sickness and came to visit him. He could not give very much advice but did write a letter to the missionary's wife, who was all alone among the Indians and had no idea what happened to her protector.

One day she saw a stranger coming on her husband's horse. He delivered a letter, written in a strange handwriting. She covered her face and was afraid to open the letter. She expected the worst. When she finally opened the letter, she found a few pencil-written notes on the bottom written by her husband. Now she at least knew that he was still alive. The letter brought her needed comfort in the wilderness.

After the ice break-up, the missionary let the farmer lift him up on his faithful horse. He held on to the front part of the saddle. The farmer with whom he had stayed all this time did not approve of him leaving yet. He was afraid that he would soon fall off his horse. Then there were only a few scattered farmhouses along the way that would take him in. When he arrived at the first river, he ventured across. His boots reached to his hips, but they still filled with water. His faithful horse brought him safely across and they stopped at the last farmhouse. The friendly old woman took him in and made a bed for him in front of the fireplace. He could not lie down, but sat up all night by the fire. The worst was yet ahead. He had to cross another river and after that there were still thirty miles through wilderness, without any human living quarters or one single Indian wigwam along the way. But the desire to get home urged him on. At daybreak he let them help him on his horse and committed his body and soul into God's hands. He often felt faint and trembled on this long, long trip, but he was able to hold himself on the horse. Just before dark he saw his log house in the distance and thanked God. He was not quite satisfied till he saw the smoke from the chimney. Now he could be sure that his life's companion was still there and waiting. She was, and both thanked God from the bottom of their hearts.

The news that he had been threatened reached his friends. They advised him to at least carry a revolver on his trips. He answered, "If I am found dead, you will know it was a dealer. No Indian will kill me." With this assurance, he quietly slept one night in the wigwam of a red man who had already killed a man. If it had not been necessary, he would not have stayed with him. However, the need was pressing, so he stayed in the name of God. The missionary slept as well as in any other wigwam. The old gray Indian was in no way friendly and seemed surprised that his guest was staying with him.

As far as the traders were concerned, they naturally were his enemies, since he interfered with the sale of *ischkudawaba* [firewater or whiskey]. They also could not ply their sometimes dishonest trade with the Indians as long as the missionary lived among them. They tried all kinds of tricks to get rid of him and to provoke and stir up the Indians against him. For instance, they heard some of the news that was printed in newspapers. These were reports of the disturbances in Germany, the Revolution of 1848. They said the white man was drawing the red man and his children to himself in order to use them in the war in Germany and then take their land from them.

The Indians told the missionary all these things and watched him carefully to see how he received the information. Calmly, he asked, "Did they say that?" "Yes," was the answer, "and it will be within six months." He replied, "That is not long. Await the time quietly and you will see if they have told the truth." The Indians waited. The lies of the traders were exposed one after another. They even concocted a tale that the Black Coat himself had escaped from Germany because his father had helped crucify Jesus Christ! The Indians could believe this story since they had no sequence of time, and if Jesus Christ was crucified fifty or five hundred years ago, that was all the same to them. However, since they told the missionary everything, they thereby showed that they had not lost confidence in him.

The traders continued to instigate the Indians against the missionary for about two years. Then the Indians no longer believed them and their confidence in the Black Coat was stronger than ever. Even the traders became ashamed of themselves, but they never became his friends. Since he did not interfere with their business except for the sale of firewater, their enmity grew less.

In the meantime, winter came again in full force. This year's winter was a severe master and reigned for a long time. The Indians considered winter an old man who sits in his wigwam by a burned-out fire and quietly smokes his peace pipe.

> I blow my breath from me,
> I breathe it on my countrymen.
> Without rule the streams stand still

61

Hard as stone turns the water.
I shake these hoary locks.
And snow covers all the meadows.
All the leaves from all the branches
Fall, wither, die and decay.

From the waters, out of marshes,
Step the wild goose and heron.
Far away to far off zones
Just one wink—they have disappeared.

And wherever my footsteps wander
All the game in field and forest,
Hole themselves in ravine and gullies.
Hard as quartz is the ground.

The Indians bring out their snowshoes and tie them to their feet. The snowshoes are a meter long and a half meter wide. The center is interlaced with sinew or tendons. They are large but light and prevent the feet from sinking into the deep snow. With these one can walk on the top of the snow, no matter how deep. It is very tiresome. But the Indians know how to walk skillfully with them. They go out when the snow is deep in order to hunt. Often their efforts are in vain. The hungry wife and children wait for them in the wigwam and lie there, bent over from cold and hunger. The winters are long and severe in these immense forests and many an Indian becomes its prey.

Everlasting, blustering winter!
Unmerciful, cold winter!
Ever thicker, ever thicker
Freezes the ice on streams and river.
Ever higher, ever higher
Falls the snow on hills and valleys
Falls the snow in thickest whirlwinds
Through the forest, around the hamlet.

From the deeply buried wigwam,
The hunter is forced to take the
        pathway.

62

Aimlessly wandering, wearing his
    thick mittens,
And immense snowshoes on his feet.
He looks for birds and game in vain.
Nowhere he sees them, in the snow he
    tramps
In the forest ghostly, sparkling glitter
Helplessly he crumbles to the ground
Dies right there of cold and hunger.
Oh how, the poor children moan.
Oh how, the women fret and worry.
Sick and starved is the body.
All around hungry breezes blow,
Hungry ever, the heavenly breath.
Hungry like the glaring wolf's eye
That now looks on him.

Only an Indian knows what it means to live through the winter in this area, therefore he counts his age by the number of winters that he lives, not the summers, but the cruel winters. The missionary was also to experience some of the hardships, though he had no foreboding.

In winter the ground is frozen. When the warm rays of the sun break forth the cold snow is melted. The trustful farmer will plant the kernels of corn. He cannot see, much less understand the mysterious strength that this little sprout of the old dried-up kernel has. The sprout breaks forth and then brings forth stalks and ears that grow, then ripen. It happened, as he had hoped. The basis for his hope is the word of God, "For as the rain and snow come down from heaven and return not thither, but water the earth, making it bring forth and sprout, giving seed to the sower and bread to the eater, so shall My word be, that goes forth from My mouth. It shall accomplish that which I purpose and prosper in the thing for which I have sent it." Isaiah 55:10,11.

This can also happen in our confused world, which is capable of being cultivated. We are sent to change it into God's garden.

Winter certainly changes many things here. The noisy festivities, the drinking orgies, dancing, the horrible beating of the witch's drums and the shrieking singing have all stopped. Most of the wigwams are empty, for their inhabitants have left for the land of Nod. This means to roam around in the forest on the winter hunt. Only a few women and a few older men stay at home. Among these are Chief Bemassikeh and his family. The good Lord arranged this, so that a small group of nineteen faithfully attended school.

In the winter silence the missionary carried on his work with the children. On Sundays a group of adults attended the service. Some of the Indians did not know when it was Sunday but came on Monday after returning from their hunt. The missionary advised them to take a stick and make a notch every day and come to church on the seventh notch. After a year of practice they could remember when it was Sunday.

When the missionary, in his catechism instructions, came to the fourth main part and had explained the doctrine of baptism, the tallest of the boys came forward and said he wished to be baptized. His name was Schegonaba,[*] meaning Thunder Feather. He was the son of Chief Bemassikeh, and was a quiet and serious-minded boy. His request was entirely unexpected. As the missionary discussed this with him, others came forward. Naturally it was necessary to get permission from the unchurched parents and relatives. To his surprise not one objected. Then a more detailed instruction of baptism was given.

In the meantime Christmas approached, and even in the wilderness it was to be celebrated in a Christian manner, in order to impress upon the children that our Father in heaven had given His greatest gift, His only Son, on Christmas day to light our life. The missionary tried to cheer the hearts of the children with gifts. For this, the diligent hands of the missionary's wife were required to make jackets, pants, shirts, aprons, kerchiefs and so forth. This meant working far into the night. The short days were filled with her regular housework.

A suitable Christmas song was to be sung, so the missionary translated Luther's song, "From Heaven above to Earth I Come" into the Chippewa language. This was not easy. The language has a unique mystery. Alexander of Humbolt is supposed to have said, "It seems to have been composed by philosophers because it is so highly developed." The language has verbs, passive verbs indicative,

---

[*]See Pollach, W. G., *Shegonaba, A Tale of Mission Work among the Chippewas.* Book and Art Publishing Company, Carl Hirst, A. G. Constance, Germany, (1929?) 94 pages.

subjunctive and also a modus potentialis, a modus desiderative and a modus reciprocus. Otherwise they have the common singularity of the Turanian language, that has the pronoun in the first person, and the plural in two forms. One includes the addressed and the other excludes him. For example, if the missionary addresses human beings with the words, "We are sinners," he must use the inclusive form, otherwise the words would mean, the white people are sinners, not the redskin. But when he speaks to God in prayer, the same word must be used in the exclusive form, otherwise being a sinner would include God.

Another peculiarity is that the verbs have different forms. After the activity has been expressed, the object it refers to has to express if the object is dead or alive. In this case the verb has three forms for the one form that we have. For example, *niwabin* means I see (actually, I am not blind). But if the sight is directed at a fixed object, then the question is, is it alive or not? In the first case it is *niwabama,* in the last, *niwabandon.* Another example, *nisagiiwe,* I love (plainly— without object), *nisagia,* I love, when this refers to a human being, *nisagiton* when it refers to a thing, etc.

The nouns as a rule are divided into a number of syllables. Death has only three syllables, but life has five. Lord and God have five. Joy, pain, etc., have six.

The thought of translating a hymn or poem and have it rhyme and then above all preserve the meaning is almost impossible. Here follow the first two lines of Dr. Martin Luther's hymn "From Heaven above to Earth I Come":

> Widi gishigong ishpiming
> Kidonjiibiotisinim
> Nimpidon tibajimowin
> Wenishishing keget nawon.

In English they translate as "From heaven above to earth I come, I bring good news to every home." The rest of the verses were translated and the children learned and sang the song with great enthusiasm.

When Christmas Eve arrived, forty Indians came. None of these had accepted Christ as their Savior yet, but they came to hear the words of Isaiah 9:6, to hear of the light that has come to all people, especially of this child, "for unto us He was born and unto us He was given."

After the sermon, there was a pause of expectation. The missionary with his wife had cut a nice cedar for the Christmas tree and had it decorated beautifully. They still had to light the candles. Then a little bell rang. The door was opened. A loud "ah" came from all sides, as they saw the brightly lighted tree before them, full of fruit, in the middle of the winter. *"Toyah!"* This was something they had never seen or expected to see. Even Chief Bemassikeh smiled and was as a child. He exclaimed that he had never found a tree like that in all his forests.

The children were now allowed to come forward, and found on the before-mentioned wilderness table on which the tree stood, nineteen tin plates. Each held cookies, an apple, and some nuts, besides the housewife's hand-made pieces of clothing. There was great joy and after they sang their Widi gishigong ishpiming, etc., once more with happy hearts, they were allowed to pick the fruit from the tree. Such was the first Christmas in the forest.

But the year was not at an end. The last day of the year brought on some tense hours, but then great happiness, for the stork stopped at the log house during the night of the last day of the year and delivered a healthy daughter.[*] Only God in heaven and the parents in the log house knew about it.

No human help was available. The missionary had to be physician and perform all the other duties. The next day the interpreter's wife, a French-Indian woman, came and willingly did what she could. Here again the Words of Scripture were proved, as when Jonathan said to his armor bearer, "It is not a big problem for the Lord to help in much or in little."

The Indian women came the very next day to see this white child. They were permitted to enter the home on the third day. They soon filled the room, not only to see the baby, but also to hold it. The mother trembled but they handled the baby very tenderly. They sat on the floor and held her on their lap. Each took a turn and it took a long while. Not satisfied that they had seen and touched her, they checked

---

[*]First child, Theodosia, born December 31, 1848. The Baierleins eventually had five children. Three girls were born in their wilderness mission home, called Bethany. One son was born in Germany, while the family was enroute from the United States to India, and another daughter was born in India.

her limbs and joints and even her fingers. They talked to each other a great deal about the child.

Now they came daily, to again see what they had never seen before. When they saw the baby bathed, they were terrified and shuddered as if they themselves had fallen into the water. The bathing of the baby had never been seen before and was an unheard-of thing. Otherwise they had the same tender motherly feelings as the white mother.

With January came the most severe part of the winter. Strong winds blew the snow through the poorly matched logs. The wind blew into the little room and cooled it even though the iron stove was red hot. The water froze in a glass by the window. A type of curtain had to be made from bedding, tablecloths, and what else was available, to hang around the bed to protect mother and child. In every way God had to help in order that both of them could survive.

Because of the condition of the rivers, the mission was isolated from the rest of the world. The missionary was not prepared for this, as it was his first winter in the wilderness with the Indians. Therefore, there was a deficient supply of food for the woman in child-bed, and nobody can create food. There was no bread or flour, no potatoes or other vegetables, nor any salt. The Indians brought venison and the red women brought a little crushed corn, of which they had very little. With this the mother's life was spared, till food could be procured. This would not be until the ice was thick enough to carry a horse and sled for fifty miles, over many streams with rapids that only freeze over when there is continuous severe cold weather.

As soon as it was possible, the missionary took off down the river to procure food, which was only to be had at the closest city, known as Saginaw. With a heavy heart he went into the store after he had wiped the tears from his eyes, for he had to have food and provisions. He had no money to buy it with and was in a strange place. After entering, he immediately admitted to the shopkeeper that he needed flour, but would not be able to pay for it. Smiling, the merchant looked him in the face and said, "You take what you need. You can bring me the money some other time. I am not worried." So without knowing it, the missionary had credit in a strange place. He hurriedly loaded his sled and returned on the long journey on the ice back to his log house.

The newborn baby was to be baptized and the Indian children

also wanted to be baptized. As they were well prepared for it, there was no reason to deny their request. Other mothers also brought their children, even though they themselves were not Christians. There were ten red children, most of whom were older, baptized at the same time as the white child, little Theodosia, was baptized. This was a great festive day in the midst of dire conditions and great isolation. Yet with happy hearts they sang,

> Dearest Jesus we are here,
> Gladly they command obeying,
> With this child we now draw near,
> In accord with thine own saying,
> That to thee it shall be given,
> As a child and heir of heaven.

Which in this strange and difficult language reads:

> Oma, sa nindaiamin,
> O Tebeningeion, Jesus.
> Chidodamang eshiang
> Ima kitikitowining
> Mab' abinoji k'dodisig
> Iu' chiwiawongomad.

Now there was a little group of Christians gathered around the missionary. This created more spirit and courage in him in the midst of this snow covered wilderness.

When the Indians shoot a mother bear, they catch the young cubs and raise them. Bear meat is delicious and compares with beef and pork. Bear hides bring a good price when sold. One time they caught three cubs and gave one to the missionary. In the beginning this queer animal brought a lot of pleasure, but later it caused a lot of trouble. As it grew it became more inquisitive, wanted to go everywhere, even on the table. With sharp claws he would pull off the tablecloth and everything that was on the table came with it. All the missionary's previous experience in education proved fruitless. Even though the animal was never mean, he had to be returned to the Indians. They knew better how to handle him.

When a bear is very small the Indian mother takes the little cub and lets it nurse or suckle on her own breast just as she would a baby, for about three years.* By that time he gets naughty and has bad manners. Then they tie him on a chain to a tall post where he can climb up and down for a pastime.

One day, when the missionary and his family visited Chief Bemassikeh, the mother lay little Theodosia on the bench next to her father, then sat down on the other side with the wife of the chief. All of a sudden there was a fierce growl. The mother screamed. The missionary instantly covered the face of the baby with one hand and grabbed the bear with the other. The bear had broken away from his chain and was about to attack the child. The chief jumped up and chained the animal again. Life in the wilderness was an ever-changing series of unexpected events for the missionary family.

---

*Three years is incredible, and Baierlein undoubtedly meant three weeks. Cubs nurse for about a month after they come from hibernation. Female cubs reach maturity at two years and males at three years. The event described was a somewhat common happening in the Indians' way of life. During hibernation the she bear gives birth to a very small cub or cubs. The cubs crawl up to the mother's teats and attach themselves there. If the mother is killed during late hibernation or soon after she emerges, the babies are still attached. Hence in order to save the cubs the Indian mothers would suckle the cubs for about three weeks, more or less. Food is always scarce during the winters, so the cubs were raised and used for meat during times of starvation, which seem to have been every winter.

CHAPTER 5

AMONG THE TREES

Horrible is the forest in winter,
Lovely though in summer.
There struggles death with life
And with life wrestles death.
Once a tree ascended from the ground,
Full of life and high aloft
Spread his mighty limbs
Full of longing, stretched them out.
Now he is lying there, tired of life,
Tossed there on the ground.
Others hurl down on top of him,
And as he, so they, decay.
Death, you have tossed them there,
Death, conqueror of nature,
Now a new life is already sprouting,
High aloft there, from the compost.
Life, you have only been asleep,
Life, you will conquer death.

Missionary Baierlein named the poor settlement Beth-any, house of poverty. The Indians called the place *Shinguagonshkom.*[*] The physical and spiritual misery was great. The missionary prayed and

---

[*] Meaning "The place of the small pine trees."

hoped that Jesus with His blessing and help would willingly enter, as He once did in the humble home of Lazarus, where He had been invited by his sisters, Mary and Martha, near that great and stately city of Jerusalem. Here the Lord, the only helper, had already entered with His blessings. Here He called the children to Him. He received and blessed them at their baptism. Who would not enjoy a place where He abides?

The gracious visit of the Lord, even in this confused world, will transform it to a paradise. The task and mission He gave to mankind is to "till the ground." Only the outcry of the confused heart will hear His voice and then by His gracious visit will transform it to a garden of God. One cannot hide from His gracious voice behind trees or in the wilderness.

The missionary had to make many trips, for he had to visit other tribes. Therefore there was a great deal to learn about the wilderness. Once, after a ten-hour ride, he reached a certain tribe and found them in the middle of a drinking orgy. That is no time to bring a message of peace. At this time the Indians are very soft-hearted and forward. When one asks them not to drink too much, they feel hurt and get angry. When drunk they are unpredictable and unrestrained. On occasions like this, the wise thing to do is to get out of their way. This happened here, but then the hoped-for night's rest was also lost. The ride had to be extended and as the sun set, shelter had to be made under a tree. The guide found a fitting spot. That is necessary for survival, and only an Indian has the right eye for the right spot in the wilderness. As they had not prepared for a lonely night in the wilderness, they had brought no material for striking a fire nor any food. The horses were tied where they could feed on tender branches of low trees to satisfy their hunger. The riders had nothing. The guide took the saddles from the horses, used his for a pillow, stretched out, covered his face and ordered the missionary to do the same, and then immediately fell asleep.

It was not that easy for a foreigner. This was altogether a new situation. First, the saddle would not fit him as a pillow. He could not rest, because he was afraid that his horse might get loose and walk away. If he dozed off, he was disturbed by unusual noises. Sometimes it was a far-off groan, then again a continuous crackling, as if a large number of sticks were broken. Then it became windy and the branches of trees rubbed together, which caused fifteen kinds of noises. A large tree fell and lodged between others and hung there, without reaching

72

the ground. Then it was very quiet. Not a sound could be heard. Then a boom! The earth seemed to vibrate. The missionary jumped up. It was only a mighty tree that fell. A prince among trees lay stretched on the garden of mold.

It is part of the skill of the frontiersmen to seek a shelter in the wilderness, where only sound and healthy trees stand, so as not to be killed by a falling tree. This skill is an instinctive part of the life of the Indian. The missionary had to learn it by experience.

The missionary learned many things in the wilderness. Many times he and his horse had to lodge under the trees by themselves. After a while, the saddle became a comfortable pillow and even the ground was not so hard and cold anymore. One thing he could never learn was to be able to sleep through the entire night. He always had to make changes by lying, sitting, or moving around.

For many, many miles around in this area, there is not one human being. Only the friendly stars wink through the thick branches at night. But much more friendly is the invisible glimpse of the guardian of Israel, who "never sleeps or slumbers" and is as near in the wilderness as if in the temple of Solomon. Weariness demands rest. The feeling brought on by the lack of meals, brings on sleep. How often we say beforehand,

> Now then I will fall asleep
> Jesus in your arms will keep.
> Your care shall be my blanket,
> Your compassion is my bed.

Everything was so new, a bit too rough and cold and unusual. At daybreak the stiff limbs were rubbed, and a little running around was required to get the blood to circulate again. The horses were saddled, and they rode on, as there was another tribe to be visited. Farther and farther they went in the quiet, lonely wilderness.

Now there was a wide river ahead of them. It was around noon. There were no rapids in sight where the water would not be so deep. The guide went into the stream on his horse. Suddenly the horse lost his footing and had to swim, but safely arrived on the other shore with his rider. Now the missionary and the guide were separated by the wide river. All horses can swim, but not all are in shape to swim with a rider on their back. The missionary's horse had never had this experience before. There was nothing left to do but to undertake the risk. He rode into the river while the guide gave orders from the other side. Loosen the stirrups! Lay the reins on the horse's neck! Lie flat on the horse's back and hang onto his mane! In the name of God, the faithful horse swam into the river with his surprised rider.

The current pushed them down the river to where they came to a place that was covered with fallen trees in such a manner that they could go no further. The animal turned his head and looked at the rider with an inquiring look as if to say, "What now?" The rider never forgot the horse's look. He was helpless to know what to do. The brave horse then followed his own judgment and swam a little further downstream and brought him safely to shore.

Now the missionary and his guide had to remove the saddles and with their flat hands rub the water from the body of the horses and wring out the padding of the saddles. While the horses caught their breath, the two men removed their own clothes and wrung them out and then put them on again. Now with wet clothes on wet horses they rode on.

That afternoon they finally arrived at the place of the Indian tribe they were seeking. They had to cross another stream before they arrived at their destination. This one was not as wide, but deeper. Small canoes lay on the shore. They were hollowed-out tree trunks and only big enough for one man. They were of the type the Indians use for fishing. It was impossible for the missionary to cross in these trough-like vessels without tipping over. They would not carry two men. This difficulty seemed to amuse the Indian and he laughed, as he expected the canoe to tip over. But the missionary took one of these nut shells, pulled it over to the other, stepped into one and held them both together while the guide stepped into the other and paddled both across.

There was no rest yet. The chief was in a bad mood. The message of peace was unwillingly heard. He was known to be an old mocker and scoffer and looked down on the white man with contempt. He said,"The white man overexerts his entire life, hunting for wealth, that in the end he cannot take with him." The Indian imagined his life to be ideal, for the Indians left the earth just as God had created it.

This chief had a friend who took the money that was paid to him yearly by the government for relinquished land, and then said, "Is this the stuff that the white man hunts and runs after?" Then, before all thepeople he threw the money into the river. This shows how much he despised the life and ways of the white man.

The chief laughed at the missionary, who then said to him, "Be not deceived, God will not be mocked. You will die like your fathers have died and I will die like mine. Then when we both appear before God's judgment, I will testify that I proclaimed God's word and the way of salvation to you and you turned me away."

"Speak to my men," yelled the chief, "they are free, I will not stop them. They can follow you if they wish." "Do you hear this?" called the missionary to the men, "you are free! Do you also intend to turn God's salvation away?" The men said, "We will have to think about it." For they were afraid of the chief.

This was the end of that visit and because no shelter was offered, there was nothing else to do but make the same trip back. They mounted the tired horses and planned to reach the next log house before dark. Horses and riders were exhausted and could not have gone much further. The missionary could not easily forget this trip as it was on his birthday. He was born April 24, 1819.

Log houses are all built alike. The larger room is living-, guest-, dining-room and kitchen. When the hungry riders arrived, they took care of the horses and then went into the house. The housewife brought out the flour, put it on the table, the only one they had, to prepare to bake the bread, while the men sat around the table. Oh no! thought the hungry missionary, it will be some time before we get something to eat. He thought of the formalities of German homes. For he never quite understood the situation in Genesis 18 verse 6, where Abraham said to Sarah, "Make ready quickly, three measures of fine meal, knead it and make cakes, while the guests wait under the trees." Here he learned it. Everything here was different from his old home. Before his eyes the flour was changed into dough, rolled flat with a water glass, and the little round rolls were twisted off. These were put in a pan and shoved in the iron oven, while the salted meat bubbled. In one half hour, the table was set and the meat together with the small hot rolls of bread that had raised in the oven were served. Also a large cup of tea made from plants that grew in the wilderness was served. Here everything was provided to make a tasty meal.

The great Macedonian boasted about his military expedition, that after a night trip, breakfast was the last meal. Otherwise supper was the tastiest. Here, both breakfast and supper were tasty. Nothing could have been better.

Again, Genesis 18:7,8 where Abraham ran to the herd and took a calf, tender and good, and gave it to the servant who hastened to prepare it. Then he took curds and milk and the calf that he had prepared and set it before them and he stood by them under a tree while they ate.

The missionary learned to understand this on different occasions. Once he and a number of Indians went up the icy river on a sled. Around a bend, they saw a deer that was trying to get away from a pack of wolves. He was caught on the slippery ice. Before the Indians had a chance to shoot at the wolves, they took off. The deer lay there. The Indians cut chunks of meat from the deer and on wooden sticks they roasted it on a hurriedly made fire. The entire procedure took less than one half-hour. The roast was done. It tasted good, even without salt, as they all were hungry.

After their evening meal in the log house, all soon retired to their deserved rest. The next morning they took off toward the missionary's own log house, where now, as almost every time, he arrived with his clothing in rags.

As long as he had a guide who was at home in the wilderness everything went well. It was more difficult when he started to go through the forest by himself. The fear of the night and being alone with his horse under a tree had long passed for him, but there were adverse situations when traveling alone.

On dark nights when there were no stars and the moon was not shining and he was unable to see the head of his horse or a white handkerchief before his eyes, he would hold one arm up for protection from the brush and courageously keep going. The horse knew the path and he only had to protect his eyes. He would hold one arm over his face and when that arm became stiff, he changed to the other. But when the horse lost the path, or if a tree had fallen across the path, which happened often, that was serious. Then, after he looked around and could not locate the path, the direction was lost. Now he would not know if he was coming or going. In that case, there was nothing to do but wait for daylight and that usually was in an uncomfortable spot.

At one time, he was forced to stop in the middle of a thick underbrush because he had lost his direction. He sat on a log, as the ground was too wet to lie down on. In order not to lose the horse he held on to the reins. He heard a far-off whispering-like noise. Is it a breeze that moves the leaves or the ripple of a rivulet? Carefully he stepped in that direction. There was a steep embankment with a little stream at the bottom. Now this helped him. He went down, put his hand in the stream to find which way the water ran. Streams always run into rivers so he knew the river was to his right. In this manner he found the proper direction he had to go.

Even during the day it is not safe to travel alone. One time the missionary decided to go around a troublesome swamp. He had heard it was possible. He happened to ride into a spot of quicksand, where a horse could sink without ever coming up again. As soon as the horse had worked himself out of one spot he immediately went in another. The missionary had to hang on to a tree so as not to sink with his poor horse. How wonderful it would have been to have seen another human being. The horse finally found solid ground. His entire body trembled from strain and exhaustion. During this incident all sense of direction was lost. It was late afternoon. There was no sun and the heavens were covered with dark clouds. There was no way to tell the four directions without a compass.

But there are other remedies. One could look at the tree trunks. Moss is thicker on the north side of a tree than it is on the south side. Another method, if a small tree is cut off straight across, the rings that tell the age of the tree are more extended on the south side than on the north side. Both are useful observations to find the right direction.

At this time both of these methods were tried, but they were not positive. When life is at stake any move in these forests is a stake not to lean on. No decision could be made. All that was left was just to sit till the pounding of the heart had subsided. Then an earnest prayer to God was offered that if He decided that this spot would be the end of his pilgrimage, He would let someone find his body, so that no faulty thoughts would be directed toward the Indians that they had murdered him. Now completely in God's hands, he relaxed. Again the signs were tried and this time they proved successful so the right direction was found.

Getting lost and wandering around in the wilderness also happened to Doctor Koch of Frankenmuth, a German colony in Michigan. Doctor Koch had to make a sick call to the new colony of Frankentrost, which is eight miles north of Frankenmuth. He arrived safely but on the way back he lost the path. He was so close to home that he could hear the St. Lorenz church bells that rang every morning and evening in Frankenmuth, but was so confused he could not find the right direction. On the fourth day an American found him and brought him home. He was almost dead. If this can be possible within eight miles, what can happen in thirty miles?

It has been proved that if one gets lost in the woods, one never goes straight ahead but keeps going in circles and always from right to left. Therefore the missionary always had the necessary foresight to align himself with two tall trees ahead of him, keep his eyes on them till he was past the first and then line up with another one. That is the only way to keep from going around in a circle.

You do not always lose a horse or ride in pitch darkness. A quiet ride through the forest during the day is delightful. One is able to collect one's thoughts, ponder and examine one's own conduct and life. This is not always possible in the busy daily life, but can happen here in the forest, where one is undisturbed. All you have to do is keep the twigs out of your eyes, which does not require much intellect. To be alone with God is always the greatest. He that has ears to hear can clearly hear God's voice among the trees in the wilderness as once they heard His voice in biblical times. The wilderness is His creation, and what an immense creation it is.

Seldom do the rays of the sun penetrate into the wilderness. It is filled with shadows, dark and full of mystery in the entire area. Yes, God is as close here as He was with Jacob on his lonely travels. To be near Him anywhere is good, not only on the high mountains, but also in the deep, lonely, and shady wilderness.

But be advised: Horrible is the forest in winter!

Every winter the missionary prayed because there is continuous and severe cold, and his only thoroughfares were the frozen rivers in this secluded forest. By the river routes he had to travel fifty miles to get supplies for his family and his Indian children for the entire year. Supplies consisted mostly of flour, which was packaged in two-hundred-pound bags, and salted meat.

Every winter he had to make a number of trips, with his little one-horse sled, to get the necessary supplies. Because of the dense forest it was necessary to use the river. There were many rapids in the river, which only froze over in the most severe weather. Sometimes one could find strong enough ice along the edge but sometimes not. Even when frozen the ice was thinner at the rapids.

It happened on one occasion that his horse broke through the ice and pulled the sled in after him. Those were dangerous moments! At these times, one could not think of oneself, above all the horse must be saved. He would have died in a few minutes in the frigid water. The life of the horse, the provisions and your own life are at stake. Those were difficult occasions and they were repeated every winter. After everybody and everything was saved, then you, soaked through and through and almost frozen, had to sit on the wet provisions and venture back toward home on the treacherous ice.

All this had to be done in a hurry, so as to catch up on lost time. The days were short, the nights long, and the log house, or any human abode, was usually far off.

When the ice is clean and smooth, the trip is fast and light and the horse trots along the path towards home. But when covered with snow, without tracks, it is like being on sand and if the horse is not in shape, then it turns into a long trip. Then there is nothing left to do but stay in the forest overnight.

In one case, the trip started out happily. Then it started to snow furiously. "Oh no," said the guide. "We will not be able to make it home today." "Why not?" asked the distrusting foreigner. "You will see before long," was the answer. And before long he saw it. The horse stopped trotting. He started to sweat and just took short strides. The deeper the snow got, the harder it was to pull the sled. Evening came and the red guide said, "Here is where we stay." "But can't we go a little further?" said the ignorant foreigner. "That will not help and we have much work to do, if we want to live till morning," was the answer.

The harness was taken off and the horse brought to shore. Dejected and unable to be of much help, the missionary stood by. The guide took an ax and looked for a certain kind of wood to chop up. This was white ash, which will burn when it is green. The missionary carried the branches over to his horse for his evening meal. That was more than his master had, who had nothing. Soon there was a big pile of chopped wood gathered together by the two of them. "That should last for three days," said the ignorant missionary. "Tomorrow morning there will not be a piece left," said the experienced guide. He was right. In the open it burned fast.

There was a night of sixteen hours ahead. It would not be light enough at eight o'clock in the morning to continue their trip on the ice. Now they had to prepare their own night's lodging under a large pine tree. First they had to shake the snow from the branches, so the heat from the fire would not melt the snow and the water drip in their faces. Then the snow was cleared from a spot to serve as a fireplace.

Next the branches of the pine tree were tossed on a pile. This was the mattress. "Now you do as I do," said the red man. He took his buffalo skin, pulled it way over his head, and rolled in it. He then lay down on the pine branches and was soon asleep. The missionary tried to imitate him, because a buffalo skin is the only thing that can protect you when it is so cold. But to him sleep did not come soon. The situation was too new for him.

Before long he was so cold that he had to turn. That happened about every hour through the night. The fire burned down and he got up and added more wood. By doing that hundreds of little sparks flew around like little stars that were pretty and at least had some life in them. Even the trees nearby were revealed by the fire. After a good evening meal and were it not quite so cold, it would all have been a lot more interesting. He crawled back into his buffalo skin.

Suddenly, through the great silence the missionary heard animal voices. They sounded half complaining, half jubilant, as they came closer. The missionary sat up, looked into the darkness, but saw nothing. He poked his companion, and asked, "What is that?" "That is nothing. They are only wolves," he grumbled under his buffalo skin. "What will they do to us?" the missionary asked. "Nothing as long as the fire burns. Do not let it go out." With that answer he turned over on his other side. After the wolves had taken a good look at the big, bright fire, they departed.

The missionary whispered:

> Now rest beneath night's shadow
> The woodland, field and meadow.
> The world in slumber lies,
> But thou, my heart, awake thee,
> To prayer and song betake thee,
> Let praise to the Creator rise.
>
> The radiant sun hath vanished.
> His golden rays are banished.
> By night, the foe of day,
> But Christ, the sun of gladness
> Dispelling all my sadness
> Within my heart holds constant sway.
> The rule of day is over

And shining jewels cover
The heavens' boundless blue.
Thus I shall shine in heaven,
Where crowns of gold are given
To all who faithful prove true.

To rest my body hasteth
Aside its garments casteth
Types of morality.
These I put off and ponder
How Christ will give me yonder
A robe of glorious majesty.
Lord Jesus who does love me
Oh, spread thy wings above me
And shield me from alarm!
Though evil would assail me,
Thy mercy will not fail me.
I rest in protecting arm.

Neither did he forget the last verse!

My loved ones, rest soundly
For God this night will surely
From peril guard your heads.
Sweet slumber may He send you
And bid His hosts attend you
And through the night watch o'r your
      beds.

They must surely have been full of worry, for they could not know why he did not come home as he had promised.

Every winter he had a couple of these nights and he almost got used to them. As long as he had an Indian with him who would find the right place for lodging for the night, and knew how to chop wood in a hurry, it went very well.

One time he was forced to stay overnight without a guide, and then things were not so good. First, he did not know how to find a good place to stay, where the white ash trees grew, nor could he tell the white ash from the other trees. Much less did he know how much wood to cut to last through the night. The wood he did cut did not want to burn. There was plenty of smoke, but no flames. This was a grave situation. He was trying to save his life.

At times the missionary was severely troubled with asthma, so he had to give up these dangerous trips alone in winter unless he had a guide.

Once when the ice seemed to be in good shape, he decided to take his wife and little daughter along on a trip. It had been a long time since his wife had seen a white face. He also had to visit an Indian tribe on Lake Huron. That was a full one-hundred-mile trip. He did not know what he was doing, and he never did it again. After all, the ice is an insecure path. Then too, much depends on the winds and weather.

For two days, everything went well. The third day they came to the Saginaw River, where it runs into Lake Huron.* Here they saw a number of sleds frozen in the ice that had broken through and were left there. The horses had died, too. The wolves had consumed part of them already. That was a powerful memento! But worse was that they could not turn around, but had to drive past these skeletons, on thin ice. It cracked at every step the horse took. On thin ice one cannot stop or drive slowly, otherwise one surely will break through. Going fast was risky, too, especially with a wife and child along. But with God's help they got over the dangerous spot.

At the mouth of the Saginaw River, the missionary met a number of Indians in an unusual occupation. They were squatted on the ice and were covered with woolen blankets and buffalo skins. They had chopped holes through the ice, and held a little shining lead fish on a hook through the hole into the water in order to catch a fish. The fish would come, grab the little fish and get caught.

Among the group was the chief of the tribe that the missionary was to visit. The chief came toward him in a slow majestic step, greeted him coldly, and asked if he had any bread with him. Gladly the missionary gave him a piece of frozen bread. He wondered what type of Indians these were because his Indians never begged. They brought him venison and bear meat, but when asked what he owed them they said that they did not want anything for it. But they did take bread, if it was a gift. Indians do not beg. That is their law, full and entire.

---

*This is now referred to as Saginaw Bay.

As they entered Lake Huron, they were met by a cold, icy north wind, the likes of which he had never before experienced. It was almost too much for the tender human beings.

The cold merciless wind was not the only thing that caused problems. Lake Huron is big and deep. At places it is three hundred meters deep and covers 65,340 qkm.* That is, Lake Huron is over four times larger than the entire kingdom of Saxony, which is less than 15,000 qkm.

In this immense lake, there are open spots, and thin ice. In places where it is very thick, it would crack, which sometimes sounds like a cannon boom. After it splits it pulls apart, then there are long open moats of water that are impossible to cross. At one of these open cracks the horse jumped across, sled and all. When they got their bearings and looked back it had already parted quite a distance. So far, in fact, that it would never have been possible to cross it again. Now they had no time to think of the danger but had to hurry to get off the ice.

How thankful they were when they arrived at the headquarters of the tribe before dark. The tribe had gathered and were happy to receive their visitors.

The day arrived to make the return trip on the same route. Things looked better, as the ice had frozen harder. On the third day of their trip it started to thaw, and they had to go thirty more miles on their own river.

This time there were three sleds. The most experienced, a trader, took the lead, followed by the missionary, his wife and child, then the guide with his sled. The rapids were still frozen over, but the ice was thin. The ice started to crack. The sleds stayed a short distance apart from each other. The trader's horse and sled broke through and sank. The trader was an active man and jumped off the sled onto the ice. The ice broke and he went down. The water is not that deep at the rapids, but deep enough for man and horse to be in danger. The man from the last sled ran up to help. The missionary stepped down. There was another crack and as the missionary turned around he saw his wife, child, and horse sink. Like lightning the Indians who lived nearby were there. One grabbed the child, the other the wife, and they

---

*Qkm=quintal square kilometers=100 km².

83

ran into the forest before the missionary with his stiff boots on the slippery ice could get to them. Now that they were safe, the horses had to be saved. They were thrashing around and were all tangled up in their harness in the icy water. After the horses were safely on the bank, the sled and provisions were taken care of.

This time there were many hands. Everybody and everything was saved. Now they had to go twelve more miles. Everybody was wet and chilled but they finally arrived at the log house. The missionary never attempted a trip like this again with his wife and child.

On another trip that the missionary and guide were on it started to snow very hard on the way home. The ice was not thick enough to carry the horses. They asked a friendly farmer to take care of the horses. They planned to walk the rest of the way home. They started out early in the morning as they knew there was a long day ahead of them. The snow was two feet deep and covered with a hard crust. This would carry the travelers three or four steps and then they would break through and go up to their knees. Then they would have to crawl back on the crust. They made no headway so they went to the river to walk on the ice. With a thick stick they checked the ice every step they took. Where it was thin, they headed for the bank and then forced their way through the snow-covered bushes and briars. It was slow progress and very tiresome.

Night came and they were still far from home. The guide said, "We have to wait till the moon comes up because we can go no farther in the darkness." They sat under a tree. Then back and forth they kept saying, "Do not go to sleep, otherwise we will not wake up!" In spite of this agreement, they both soon were stretched out in the snow. How long they slept they did not know. The moon had risen high above the trees and was shining brightly in their faces. The missionary was surprised that he had fallen asleep. He woke his guide, who would have preferred to sleep a little longer.

Their limbs were stiff and they could not turn their necks. How they wished that they could sleep just a little more. The danger was great so they headed for the ice and went on. Neither one spoke. They had hardly enough strength to walk, let alone talk. In addition they were half asleep.

They finally arrived at the log house. It took them a number of days to recover. The missionary often had to take the place of a doctor at home and sometimes on a trip. The American doctor did not seem to be able to find a cure for the dreaded forest fever, which plagued people for months. The missionary received a number of calls for help. He always was known as Kitschimuschkikiwinine, or the Great Medicine Man among the Indians. Surprisingly, he received this title from an Indian witch doctor who lived by the river and was sick. When his own remedy did not help, he was moved to call the missionary. The missionary came and looked and found that he only needed an ordinary emetic. The missionary went home and had an Indian deliver a small bottle of medicine to the witch doctor. It looked like clear water, without taste or odor. He was supposed to drink half of it immediately and if it did not help in half an hour, to drink the other half. The witch doctor thought he was being made fun of. He said, "Do I not have enough water here in the river, that he has to send me this little bottle of water, and then drink only half of it?" He then drank the entire dose, thinking it was only water. He soon changed his mind. He started to vomit but immediately felt better. He said, "He must be a great medicine man, that with a small bottle of clear, clean water, he can cause such a cure."

After this the missionary was called by other Indians to help heal wounds, pull teeth, and solve other problems.

These are some of the noteworthy things that happened to the missionary in the wilderness. In the summer, when alone on trips among the trees, when the horse and rider became tired, they stopped and spent the night. Fear and loneliness did not bother him any more. The long winter nights, of course, were serious, especially when it froze and the temperature would occasionally drop to ten to twenty degrees below zero. After a while you get used to this and you prepare for it. Sleeping under trees happened every winter. But when you have an Indian guide at your side, a good fire at your feet, and a good buffalo skin to wrap around you, it is not so bad. Each of these incidents and each night's lodging was different from the other. But to write about all of them is not the aim. A few experiences are enough to show the life of a missionary in the wilderness. The trying conditions call for good, healthy, dedicated messengers, who have complete trust in the Lord.

He will protect you and keep you wherever He sends you. Even in the middle of the wilderness.

CHAPTER 6

THE NEW HOME

There are troubles in the wilderness
And dangers never thought of,
Wandering through the pathless wilds,
To show wild men the right path!
Speak, like no book teaches,
Learn to speak to the wild ones.
And to those that live only for today,
Prepare them for eternal life.
Only with God's help can that be done.
Only from God comes courage and wisdom.

The log house, built in great haste, was indeed a poor home. It was a severe winter and a miracle that all survived. One night a fire broke out. The severe cold weather and deep snow made it almost impossible to go for help. "Save the wife and child and leave the house to us," called the men who came running, ready to help. "What then, and where will we go?" This was the missionary's first thought. He crawled up into the loft, where the fire was, to see if there was any possibility of putting the fire out and saving the house. It was fortunate that there was no wind and plenty of snow and water. The fire was quickly doused.

All this passed and spring came and the hardships were soon forgotten. But it was soon evident that the site where the log house stood was not suitable. The water from the melted snow overflowed to the low spot where it stood. There was nothing left to do but to look for a site that was on higher ground. There was no other house available.

Moving houses is not unusual in America. The lighter, so-called frame houses are put on rollers and pulled along streets. Even two-story houses with all the furnishings in them are moved. On Lake Huron, a house was moved twelve miles on ice. When near the new site, the house was taken to the shore and to the selected location. This cannot be done with log houses because the logs are only laid on top of each other and the house would fall apart.

The missionary and his family then had to move into a wigwam again, also a tent was put up that served as a workplace and bedroom. The log house was taken apart, and the logs moved to the new site, then rebuilt. The first cabin was so low that the tall missionary could not stand up straight, so a few more logs were added to make it higher. Otherwise it was the same as the former building.

As the family grew, because of more Indian children, a little room was added to serve as a kitchen. It was a slow project as there was very little help available. It required many trips and sometimes things came to a standstill. September came with the equinoctial storms [tornadoes]. That was something else the missionary had not experienced before. As the rustle in the treetops started the missionary's wife suddenly screamed for her husband, who was in the tent. A large black snake was boldly coiled under the basket crib of the child. As the missionary ran toward the log house, the storm broke and twisted. After he left the tent the storm tore it apart. The books and bed flew all over, then the pouring rain soaked everything. A half-Indian ran up and yelled, "Save the wife and child. I will take care of the tent." But go where? In the log house! As they headed for the log house the half-Indian yelled, "Not in the house, the logs will fall on your head." The roof was not finished. The parents kept going with their child in the basket till they arrived at a wigwam and found shelter.

Most severe storms come in the spring in this area, but occasionally appear in the fall. To the missionary, as with so many other things, these were new and unknown to him. The snake that had crawled under the crib did not mean to do any harm, it only wanted to find shelter from the approaching storm that it somehow knew was coming. The animals have a distinct anticipation of a coming storm.

The animals that live free in the forest have more sense than those that live in a barn. In the wilderness, barns and feeding in barns were not yet heard of.

For example, the horses of the missionary were free to roam in the forest. They knew exactly where to go for food. They always looked well fed, round and shiny. Sometimes it took days to find them. Only an Indian could find, catch, and then ride them home.

About every two weeks the horses would come back on their own. They would come to the log house, and put their noses on the windows, to make known their arrival. That was when they required salt, which is necessary for their health. They would lick up a whole platter full. They would neigh or whinny loud, as if to say, "Thank you." Then with a few lively leaps, they again disappeared into the forest. Even in winter, through deep snow they had to forage for their own food. Only when they were needed often, they were not allowed to leave, because it was so hard to find and catch them.

Finally the walls and roof of the house were completed. A lot of inside work had yet to be done. The missionary took a lot of pains, and brought boards home on his little sled. Now he had to get busy with saw, plane, hammer and nails. The only thing he knew how to do was to saw a board. He knew very little about how to use a plane. But it is surprising what a person can do when he has to.

He made a bed so they did not have to sleep on the ground anymore, a fairly decent table, a writing desk, chairs, and stools. He also nailed a wardrobe to the log wall. There were a lot of blisters on his hands, but they disappeared after a while. They had to, for there was harder work ahead.

After the most important work was done inside, he started outside. The trees closest to the house had to be cut, so they would not fall on the house when a storm came. Ground had to be prepared around the house for a garden in order to raise corn, potatoes, beets, and other vegetables for his growing family.

Adam Ricked, a German man, was supplied by the Lutheran mission board of Frankenmuth, but he knew less about clearing the land than the missionary. He would accomplish very little when alone. Much time and energy was required for cutting down the trees and preparing the piles of brush. He had to learn how to swing an ax, but before long was not afraid to tackle the largest trees. The branches had to be trimmed off and then the logs cut up into pieces, so they could be rolled into high piles. The branches were carried and piled together in big heaps. When dry, they would be burned.

There were several smoldering fires on the north and west sides of the house. Toward the river it had already been cleared. After school was out the missionary worked at clearing the area with his broadaxe, poked the fire now and then, and added other brush. These were happy days. The fires smoldered for weeks. He was busy far into every night. This project went on every summer, till finally he had cleared eight acres.

With the fires many black snakes appeared. These were usually killed. Snakes are hard to kill, unless their head is crushed. Otherwise they slither away. The missionary made it his duty to kill all those he could find and throw them into the fire.

One snake he did not kill. It was not by the fire, but on one of his solitary trips. His horse suddenly stopped and would not move. He could see no obstacle so he forced him on. The horse leaped high, as if jumping over a high stump. The missionary turned around to see what the problem was. There on the path was a rattlesnake, ready to strike and making the peculiar rattle with its tail. Gladly would he have killed that one, but was afraid that if he dismounted, it would strike him or the horse. The bite of a rattlesnake is deadly for man or beast. He was alone, so he thought it best to let this poisonous reptile live, no matter how much he would have liked to rid the world of snakes.

The land where the forest had been cleared was not ready to be plowed. There were still too many stumps and thick roots. In some areas it is easy to hoe. It was good ground and it produced good crops.

It was with pleasure that the missionary went with his red children to dig potatoes. Under each bush was found a full nest of potatoes. Such rich harvest as this could not be found in Germany. The beets, carrots, and corn grew very well. The corn planted in June was above the missionary's head in August.

The corn stalks were fodder for the animals. Later there were cows, chickens, and pigs. The horses were fed corn instead of oats, when they had to work. When they did not work they were not fed. They did not mind, they found their own. In the winter they were put to work pulling the sleds to get supplies and in the summer were used as riding horses.

The missionary also wanted a garden by his house. He was used to one from his childhood and that hobby has stayed with him even in his old age. He leveled the ground, dug out the stumps and made his garden. It had a little path through it. He planted fruit trees from the seeds his wife had saved from fresh fruit. Also he planted wild strawberries and wildflowers.

Besides physical work, there was also a lot of spiritual work to be done. The missionary still had a lot more to learn of the difficult language and this without books or teachers. The French-Indian who was his interpreter had no idea what grammar or syntax meant. However, he could translate words and sentences.

There was activity in the log house, especially during school hours. Four languages were spoken daily, and on occasions four others were read.* On stormy days when the students and family were confined indoors, one could hear several languages.

Church and school services started again. The old chief kept making his occasional visits. He was a dignified old master. He could step humbly or speak like a commander-in-chief. He was inclined toward Christianity, but did not become involved. When the missionary approached him for a heart-to-heart talk, he would say, "Do not think that I do not think about it. I do that when I rest and when I am alone in the forest. I well remember what you said in your very first sermon. But it takes time for me to work it out."

Once when the missionary was preparing for a long trip to attend a Lutheran Missouri Synod conference, the chief heard that he had to travel through Detroit, where the government-appointed Indian agent was stationed. He said to the missionary, "I will give you a message, to deliver to the Government agent and have him send it to the Great Father, the president of the United States." This the chief did. The evening before the trip, he spoke for two hours in a loud, strong voice, always addressing the president. Among other things, he said, "Do you remember what you said when you asked for my land? I will remind you. I will speak to you so it will go to your heart. You said you would take care of me. That I would have no more problems. My children would be clothed and I would not be able to recognize my wife because of the beautiful clothes and jewels that she would be wearing. But as often as I look at her," he turned and looked at his wife, who sat beside him, "I still know her very well, and I do not see any beauti-

---

*German, English, Chippewa, Polish, French, Latin, Hebrew, and Greek.

ful dresses or jewels. You have taken my land. I have received nothing for it or at least as much as nothing. Now I am old and there is little that you can do for me, for soon I will go to my fathers and to the fathers of the fathers. But here is my son, do not forget him."

He spoke in great earnest for a long time. The missionary's heart ached. The chief obviously thought such things were as simple in the government as they were in the forest. He did not realize that the "Great Father" had only four years to rule and then gave the position to another Great Father. That it was not the same one that he had made the agreement with. At this change, all officers and Indian agents were also changed. Under this system it is easy to make promises and easy for the agents also to take advantage of the situation and not fulfill the promises when in four years others would occupy their positions. It is not easy to make the Indians understand. They think the Great Father was indeed the chief as long as he lived. Then his son would become chief and conduct himself in the same manner as his father.

The Indians possessed extensive hunting reservations, where the white man squeezed in and encroached upon the Indians' rights. They were not satisfied to spread out step by step, but moved in large leaps. Even today the state of New York contains great stretches of uncultivated and uninhabited land. Families travel hundred of miles from their white neighbors and settle on new homesteads wherever it is suitable for living. Often this is in the midst of the habitat of the Indians. They establish themselves wherever they please when the Indians are not present. Indians are often not at home, as they travel great distances to fish and hunt. So the white men took over and built wherever it suited them, sometimes far from each other, while each claimed as much land as possible. When the Indians returned and found these intruders, as they considered them, had approached too near to their homes, they tried to drive them away. They burned their isolated log cabins and killed the occupants. There was a great cry about the cruelty of the Indians. But they were merely doing in their way what we likewise do today. The forest for ages had been the hunting grounds of their fathers. They looked upon the white men as invaders. The government had promised the white man would not interfere with them. He came, however, avenged himself and killed the Indians. In order to prevent this evil, the government sought to induce the Indians to sell their lands. The price often was a mere pittance, since they received only the interest, as it were, which was to be paid annually. The government officials tried to settle affairs, but the decisions were often hard, ruthless, and unfair to the Indians. They thought they were defending their innate rights. Finally they had to succumb to the laws of the higher government. Only with pensive melancholy can one look back on the many years of war.

Naturally the missionary could only promise Chief Bemassikeh to give the message to the agent in Detroit. That meant he had to repeat what the chief had said so he could send it to the president in Washington. The missionary departed the next morning. He rode his horse up to a farmer's home and there he put it in a fenced-in pasture with the farmer's horses. He then left in a mail coach to go to the railroad, and then on to Detroit. There he called on the Indian agent and repeated the speech of the chief. The agent said, "What should we do then? We get a fixed sum of money. We have to divide this among the different tribes and chiefs. During the transaction some of this is used before it is divided. If we hand them the money, they spend it on drinking orgies or are cheated out of it. So instead we buy them woolen blankets, ammunition, guns and such things. What is left they get in cash."

This all sounded well, but it is certain that each year more money sticks on the fingers of the many hands it has to go through. In the end the Indians get very little and every year they receive less and less.

From Detroit he traveled by steamer and railroad to the far-away synod assembly in St. Louis, Missouri. As he bought his ticket he found that all steamer and railroad tickets are only half-price for all clergymen and other religious church workers that travel on official duty. He admitted that he was a clergyman and was traveling to the synod conference. It has been said that America is the land that worships the dollar, but again there is no land that is as charitable as America. Doctors usually say, "We do not charge the clergymen."

At the time of the meeting of the Synod of Missouri, of which the missionary was a member, it was only a few years old. There were only pastors there. There were no old men among them. Dr. Walthers, president of the Lutheran Missouri Synod, was only in his thirties, but there was life and determination, faith and love in him and among the others present. The ten days of meetings were not only extraordinarily refreshing for each one of the servants of the Lord, but also administered a great blessing on the congregation.

The members of the St. Louis congregation graciously furnished lodging for all synod officials, pastors, teachers and elders. Each host asked for more than one guest. During the synod conference, invitations came in from different congregations to have the synod meet at their church the following year. It was an emotional time for all. Those who furnished shelter and those who were sheltered were blessed by each other.

There was not enough time for all the business and problems that needed to be discussed at this time. There were many long presentations that had to be discussed. They were all doctrinal and vital questions about the true doctrine according to God's word and the Lutheran symbols. Everyone was allowed to freely express his thoughts. The church elders stepped forward and gave their opinions. Usually Dr. Walther expressed his thoughts before closing the sessions.

After fourteen days, the missionary, strengthened and pleased, returned to Saginaw. When he arrived at the farm he found that his horse had jumped over the fence and walked away. This was disquieting news. He asked people all over to look for his horse, then borrowed one and rode home. Everybody had looked and he had given up all hope of ever finding his faithful animal again. Suddenly, one evening after the missionary had arrived at home, he heard a familiar noise. The horse announced his coming home with the usual nose rubbing on the window. He was home and demanded his salt.

The horse had traveled twenty miles* through different farms, had to cross two rivers and then thirty more miles through thick dense wilderness to reach home. It seemed proper that he was proud of his accomplishment, for he was happy and in good humor.

---

*From Saginaw to where Midland is now located is about twenty miles. The trail was on the east side of the Tittabawassee River. The fording place was just above the mouth of the Chippewa River. Three miles west the Chippewa River had to be forded to reach the trail on the south side of the Pine River. It was thirty miles from the Pine-Chippewa River junction to the Bethany Mission site.

CHAPTER 7

DEATH AND THOUGHTS OF DEATH

By death encompassed, in the midst of life,
Where do we look for help and receive mercy?
To you dear Lord alone.
Now we are sorry for our sins Lord, that annoyed you.

Holy Lord God! Holy powerful God!
Holy merciful Savior! you eternal God!
Let us not sink
Into the bitter perils of death.
Lord have mercy upon us.

We well know that death may take us at any hour. How often it happens that death unexpectedly takes a friend or someone in our family.

Old Chief Bemassikeh often spoke of death,[*] that he soon would go to his father and his father's father. When death finally came, it surprised everyone. The chief leaned toward Christianity. He intended to become a Christian, but the struggle in his own mind was never completed. Death came unexpectedly and took him. Even as he was dying, he leaned toward the Lord by ordering his wife and children to become Christians. He added that he would have become one, if he had lived longer.

---

[*]The chief died May 23, 1850.

The sad part was, the missionary happened to be away on a long trip when death called the chief. Maybe if the missionary had been there in his last days, the chief would have made the decision and would have died a Christian.

Returning from his trip, the missionary was still on his horse when he heard the news, "Bemassikeh is dead!" That was a heavy blow because he loved the old man. Now in his last hours, not once was the missionary able to be with him in his wigwam. Again and again he thought about this with a heavy heart. After forty years, it still grieves him deeply, that he did not spend more time with him, show him more love, and that his last days had to be so far from him. With great sorrow and mourning his people buried their beloved chief. For a long time they ate their meals at his grave.

In such a death there is much sorrow. The women break out in a peculiar wailing. One might call it a howling, which penetrates to the marrow of the bones of the listeners. That is the mourning of those who have no hope. Quietly and motionlessly, the men sit around the dying man. Their faces show deep earnestness and not a muscle moves. When the final death struggle comes, the women cover the face of the man. When he is dead one of the men cries out, *"ashi,"* it is done. The men quietly rise, take their already prepared hunting guns, and shoot a number of times in his honor. Thereby they want to announce the arrival of the dead man to the kingdom of the dead.

The closest relatives and close friends blacken their entire faces. Others only paint one side of the face, while some only a few black stripes. This depends how close the friendship was. Slowly they walk to the burial grounds, where the grave is to be dug. The body is dressed in the man's best clothing. Material for striking a fire, cooking kettles and supplies of food are put in place. The body is wrapped. The women now approach and whisper secrets into the ears of the departed. These are greetings to the fathers, mothers, children, and friends in the beyond. The grave is lined with tree bark. The body is lowered into the grave and covered with tree bark so the earth does not touch the body. The grave is then filled with earth. In the meantime, the witch doctor sings his piercing songs and beats on a drum.

Small tree trunks are prepared and laid around the grave to form a miniature log house. This is about two feet high. At the head of the grave an opening is made in the little house which serves as a door for the soul when it wants to visit the body. The relatives come every day and have their meal at the grave. They light a fire and burn the food, making it invisible. In this way the food is transported into the invisible world into which the dead man has entered. Gradually the meals at the grave become less and less frequent, then once a year and finally are discontinued. Then the deceased is forgotten as we all forget the dead!

The deceased still has a long trip ahead of him in this world toward the far west. That is the place they consider their paradise. It is not an easy trip.

The missionary once had an interesting talk about death with a couple of older Indians. They had stayed after the church service on Sunday. The missionary supplied them with tobacco. As they smoked he had a long visit with them and talked about death. He asked, "What do you believe happens to a person after they die?" One old Indian answered, "When the chief reached the banks of a river in the west* he had to stop. One evening after dark a group of Indians, who were also going west, gathered together. There were whites there and they gave the Indians all kinds of gifts. However, the [dead] Indians could not accept the gifts unless they were passed through the fire." "But," interrupted the missionary, "what I really wanted to know is, what do you believe happens after you die?" "That is it," answered the old Indian. "One time a Frenchman had an Indian wife. They lived happily together. Because of his fur-trading business he was transferred further west. He left his wife behind. One evening he met a woman who was exactly like his wife. He kept away from her and would not have anything to do with her. She really was his wife. After he had left on his mission she died and arrived in the west before he did. One evening many Indians came to him. They were loaded down with good furs. He did a good business and soon was rid of all his wares. But he had to throw each piece into the fire first. Otherwise the Indians would not accept them. At dawn, the trader checked his furs and they had all disappeared. They had all turned to tree bark. For dead Indians are only visible at night and their goods are only goods at night."

"But how do you know it will be the same when you die?" asked the missionary. The old man answered, "Once there were two good friends who were related, they loved each other very dearly. They

---

*The Algonquin Indians, of which the Chippewa are a part, believe at death the soul remains nearby for a period. At night they appear life-like. After a short stay in the area they go west to the banks of the river, which they have to cross to get to paradise.

promised each other that if one of them died, the other would be buried with him. It really happened. One died, and nothing could change the other's mind to break the promise. A large grave was dug and both were buried. Everybody worried that the earth would crush him. Soon the living one fell asleep. When he awoke it seemed he was in a wigwam with the dead one. There they lived a long time, even hunted with each other. But only during the night was the dead one able to shoot anything. Finally the dead one said, 'Listen to me, tomorrow I will get a lot of visitors, they will take me away. But this time you cannot go with me. Therefore I would advise you to return to your living brothers. Tomorrow people will come and open the grave.' That happened. The living one heard a noise above him that came closer and closer. Finally all the earth and tree bark was removed. The people said to each other, 'This one has his eyes open, he is still alive.' 'Certainly I am alive,' and he stepped out of the grave. He then told them of all his experiences."

"Where do you get these stories from?" asked the missionary. "My forefathers told me," answered the old man. "Their forefathers told them, and so it goes back to the man it happened to."

Now said the missionary, "I will tell you what God says will happen after we die. Here in this world everybody builds his wigwam where he pleases and lives as he chooses. In the life to come God will assign us the place where we will gather and will have to stay. Only God is able to say what will happen there and what he will do with us. For He has said, 'When the Son of Man comes in His glory, and all the angels with Him, then He shall sit on His glorious throne. Before Him will be gathered all the nations and He will separate them one from another as a shepherd separates the sheep from the goats. He will place all the sheep at His right hand, but the goats to the left. Then the King will say to those at His right hand, "Come, oh blessed of my Father, inherit the kingdom prepared for you from the foundation of the world. For I was hungry and you gave me food. I was thirsty and you gave me drink. I was a stranger and you welcomed me. I was naked and you clothed me. I was sick and you visited me. I was in prison and you came to see me." Then the righteous will answer him, "Lord, when did we see you hungry and feed you or thirsty and gave you drink and when did we see you a stranger and welcomed you, or naked and clothed you? When did we see you sick or in prison and visited you?" And the King will answer them, "Truly, I say to you, as you did it to one of the least of these my brethren, you have done it to me." Then he will say to those on his left hand, "Depart from me, you cursed, into eternal fire prepared for the devil and his angels. For I was hungry and you gave me no food. I was thirsty and you gave me no drink. I was a stranger and you did not welcome me. I was naked and you did not clothe me. I was sick and in prison and you did not visit me." Then they will also answer, "Lord when did we see thee hungry or thirsty or a stranger or naked or sick or in prison and did not minister to you?" Then he will answer them, "Truly, I say to you, as you did it not to one of the least of these, you did it not to me." and they will go away into eternal punishment, but the righteous into eternal life" (Matthew 25:31–46).

These words made a deep impression on the Indians. The old man and his friends expressed unmistakable numbness. A long deep silence followed. Finally the old man collected his thoughts and said, "Yes, that is so. Years ago, many Indians let themselves be baptized and became Christians. Once a praying Indian, that is what the Indians call a Christian Indian, died. That means the soul left his body, but there was still a little breath left in his body. So they did not bury him right away. After some time he revived and told them what had happened. He said, 'I was dead. When I arrived at the heaven of the white people they would not let me in. They said, "This is for white people only, red men do not belong here." So I came back. After some time the same thing happened again.'

"When he revived, he said, 'I was dead again and when I came to the Indian heaven in the far west, they also turned me away and said, "You are a praying Indian. We do not pray here, leave." Therefore I came back again. Nobody would accept me. I think the best thing to do is to give up praying and live the life in the old Indian way so I will be able to enter the Indian heaven.' This he did and when he died the third time, he did not return. Since then our people have been afraid of baptism, because they lose the heaven of the red man, and are not able to reach the heaven of the white man."

The missionary said, "Did you not tell me that the Indian was not quite dead the first and the second time?" "Yes," said the old man, "he was hardly breathing, therefore he was not buried." The missionary said, "Then he was only dreaming all this time. I have often preached about your dreams in my sermons. The *matschimamito* [devil] only deceives you, to keep you from God's ways and eternal life."

In return, the old man said, "There are also many white men that are bad, and oppress and grieve the Indians."

"Without doubt, there are such," answered the missionary. "There are worldly minded people found among all peoples that have no hope for eternal bliss in yonder world. They try to get their share in this life and among that is money. Money is sometimes hard to get in an honest way. So they turn to crooked ways. Then by falsehood and deceit they reach their goal. They then think they are blessed, which actually is not a blessing.

"I have never said that you should adjust to the white man's ways but that you should adjust to what God asks and orders you to do. Just now, you heard me say that all people will gather, the white, the red and the black. He will divide them. The wicked will go to eternal agony, but the good will go with Him to eternal bliss, red, black or white. God is no respecter of persons."

This ended the interesting conversation. The Indians, like children, enjoy and believe nursery tales. Their heart is like the wilderness. First the trees have to be chopped down, then the ground has to be cultivated before the seed is able to grow. Even then there will be stumps with their many deep roots that stay in the ground for years and hinder regular plowing and seeding. They are noble children of nature, to which they maintain their loyalty. They cannot be compared with the beggarly ways of men of other races on whom the Indians look down.

Now these are the wigwam tales and fables and what the Indians think happens after they die. This is what they believe.

When man dies, he still spends some time in his grave, for it is hard for him to leave his old home. But finally he has to begin his long trip to the west. For this, it is necessary to supply him with kettles, materials for starting fires, and food. He also has to have new shoes on his feet. At times the trip is difficult but at times it is not. When he gets to the far west he finds a wide river in front of him and he cannot go any further.

On the other side are the homes of the blessed ones. He can almost hear their shouts of joy. But he is not there yet. The river is deep and wide. Suddenly, all by itself a little canoe floats up to him so he can risk the trip across. But the little canoe is hewn out of stone, not wood. It can easily carry the man's light soul across but not his sins. They are too heavy, hence he does not dare to try it. If he does he may sink or get lost. He cannot go back nor can he go forward. So he may never reach the land of bliss.

Now the Indian does not know what he, as a sinner, can do about his problem. So consequently he remains a slave of the fear of death as long as he lives. So this all fits together and makes sense. The Indian really does not want to move to the far west, even though his paradise is there. This has already caused the government many wars in trying to get the Indians to move west, even a few days journey toward the west.

Yes, it is a pitiful and deplorable situation among all people that live without any real hope. There is always worry and fear, but death finally comes and they have no hope.

A full life here in this world, then eternal bliss can be attained only through Jesus Christ our Savior. He can span the wide river carrying our sins so we can be reconciled to God.

Death also came quickly to the log house. A student, sixteen-year-old Pauline, a quiet Christian girl who was sick with tuberculosis, was getting weaker. The missionary noticed that death was near. He looked for a suitable place for a cemetery. He felt that he could not bury his Christians among the unchurched. He cleared a plot of ground on a little hill, built a fence around it and erected a tall cross. Then he made a straight path from the gate to the cross. In this cemetery he soon placed the Indian maiden, Pauline. No coffin was available. She had to be buried according to the Indian custom. She was clad in a white dress and the body enclosed by tree bark. The children sang:

> Wenen gekendang n'dishquasewin!
> Majiosewon gishigodong:
> Nibowin biginibimagut
> Chishquaseg nimbimatzwin:
> O Christ, Kibaqusenimi
> Mano chimins nigoian

That is:

> Who knows when death may overtake
>   me!
> Time passes on, my end draws near.
> How quickly can my breath forsake
>   me!
> How soon can life's last hour appear!

101

My God, for Jesus' sake, I pray
Thy peace may bless my dying day.

All the Indians who were not away from home came to attend the first Christian burial. It was so different from the heathen customs. There was no weird singing by a witch doctor, no drums, no drunken men, no piercing wailing by the women. Only the quiet sorrowful tears of the white as well as the red occupants of the log house. The graveside service was listened to attentively. Here a young life was called, not to go to the far west, but to be forever with the Lord. With the Lord who Himself took over our sins and therefore is the only sure way to our Father in heaven. Not in a stone canoe that will sink under the weight of our sins.

Here the missionary showed them the difference between those that serve the Lord and those that do not serve the Lord. He compared the mourning of those that have no hope with those that are sure of their hope of everlasting life and a joyful resurrection.

As the body was lowered into the grave and the missionary threw the first handful of earth into the grave with the words, "Ashes to ashes, dust to dust" and so forth, a deep groan was heard. A very old blind woman completely broke down and started to weep. Then she repeated the words,"Ashes to ashes, dust to dust." She was the grandmother of the deceased. She was a hardened old heathen who had often turned away from His mercy and grace. Now her stony heart was broken. Soon after, she came to attend instructions and was baptized. She was not the only one that came after witnessing the burial of Pauline.[*] Later, more came to instructions and were also baptized.

---

[*]See Appendix III, grave marker number 1.

CHAPTER 8

IN THE SCHOOL

Now a schoolhouse, newly built
Was the kikinoamading [classroom].
Happily the children came,
Learned to read and pray.
Men of stature also came,
Considerate and ready for advice.
Heavy problems on their chest,
A new life to attain.
New life, new ways,
New homes, down here and above.

The log house had become too small to serve as a home, school, and meeting place. Therefore a schoolroom was added to the house. The new addition was twenty feet long and sixteen feet wide. In this room divine services were also held until the church was built. More order was brought into the school but there were still many difficult problems to face.

The only school books were in the English language. Although the children learned to read English to a certain extent, they could not speak it fluently. This took a lot of time and was not easy. The Chippewa language was spoken in the settlement. Naturally in the log house German was spoken. Some learned enough German so they could speak in German. But what good was the German language to them in this country? The natural solution was to teach the children to read in their native language first. After that they could learn as many languages as they wanted to. But for this there had to be books, and these did not exist.

The missionary had to get busy and write a school book in the Chippewa language and then have it printed.[*] Again, this was not easy. The pronunciation of the English alphabet made instructions difficult. He then used the Latin alphabet, but kept the English *j* for *dsch,* the *ch* as *tsch,* and the *sh* as *sch.* There is no *r* or *l* in the Chippewa language. This booklet was made in two parts with an appendix. Part I was the spelling book with the English translations of the Chippewa words. Part II was the reader. The lessons were taken from the Bible. They included the creation, creating man, paradise, the first sin, and the results of sin, the flood, Noah and his sons, Abraham, Sodom and Gomorrah, the patriarchs, Moses, a summary of God's laws and the object of the laws.

There were more lessons from the New Testament, especially about our Savior Jesus Christ, from His birth to His resurrection and ascension. It closed with a summary of the Epistles such as,"Death where is thy sting, Hell where is your victory?" The appendix included a number of hymns and prayers. After being written, the book had to be printed. The missionary then went to Detroit, the capital of Michigan. This trip was 150 miles. Since he had to stay in Detroit till the book was printed and bound, his family went with him. A man was left behind to take care of the house and school. The Indians were worried that the missionary might not come back. It did take longer than he had planned. The printer in Detroit had very little knowledge of printing and because of the Indian language many corrections had to be made.

Finally the book was finished. The missionary and his family packed and were on their return trip. Because they came so close to the German colony of Frankenmuth, on their trip they stopped there. They were duly welcomed at the parsonage. While there the maid who worked at the parsonage asked the pastor and his wife for permission to serve the mission family. There was astonishment over this request and her sudden determination to live among the Indians. Pastor and

---

[*]Baierlein, E. R., Okikinoadi-mezinaigan, Spelling and reading Book in the Chippewa Language. Daily Tribune Book and Job Print. (1852) Detroit, Michigan. 144 pp.

Mrs. Roebellin granted her wish. As the wife of the missionary could use extra help she was gladly accepted. She was a faithful and Christian helper, capable and unselfish. We will speak of her later.

Now the wife had help. They left Frankenmuth and continued up the river in Indian canoes, that is, hollowed-out tree trunks. On the way they had to set up a camp under the trees. This was the first time that the children had experienced this, although the wife had done it with the missionary before. Now it was summer and the nights were shorter.

Finally they reached the village. The Indians showed all the love and esteem that they were capable of. As soon as it was made known that the missionary family was coming home, some of the Indians climbed onto the roof of their dwellings to get the first glimpse of the returning family. Others walked to meet them and when they met they jumped into the river to shake hands with them. They pulled the canoes to the landing where a crowd of men and women, Christian and heathen, stood to welcome them back.

Before they had time to think, they had emptied both canoes and everyone was happy to carry something up the hill and enter the log house. The children shouted with joy as they were carried on the shoulders of the men. As the mission family came along they had to shake hands with everybody. There was such a crowd they could hardly get inside. They had to greet them all over again. The children could not have been happier when their own parents returned from a long trip, than these Indians were on the return of the missionary family. All acted alike, young, old, Christian and heathen.

Nothing was mentioned about killing the missionary any more. Some of them would rather have been killed themselves, before they would let any harm come to the missionary or his family.

More enthusiasm and attention was now shown for learning. It was much easier with the newly printed book. With each word, the children recognized something in their own language or surroundings and beside it there was an English translation. Now they were able to read the Bible stories about paradise, patriarchs, and so forth. With the New Testament their pleasure was complete. They were not satisfied to read the stories for themselves, they enjoyed reading them to their parents and friends. Therefore their eyes were opened. New thoughts came into their simple life. They loved to memorize the hymns and sang them to the German melodies with great delight. Later, the faithful maid told Pastor Loehe[*] in Germany how the Christian hymns sung by the Indians made her work much easier. The new booklet introduced new life into the settlement for both young and old.

On the whole, the life of the Indians is well disciplined and orderly. The men supply the family with game and fish. The women raise and harvest the corn in the fall and make maple sugar in the spring. They tan the skins of the deer with water, smoke, and hard work. Moccasins are made of the leather for themselves, their husbands and children. These are nicely embroidered and decorated. They also make clothing for the family. So there is always plenty of work. This is always good, for it keeps a person out of trouble.

At the same time there was not always sunshine in the wigwam. Then the men knew what to do. They never quarreled. If a quarrel threatened, the man quietly took his gun and went on a long hunt. When he returned, after eight days or so, all was forgotten and love was fresh and young. The wife knew this would happen and seldom let things go that far.

The women were rather independent. When necessary they could speak quite well. One evening when all the men were absent the women came to the log house. The leader, without delay, turned toward the pastor and spoke in well chosen words. She said, "You see a group of foolish women, but our men are absent and we hear a report that certain people intend to drive us from our lands and will sell them soon at an auction in Saginaw. We do not know whether this is true or not. But they say it is true. We have come to receive an intercession" and so forth.

The pastor quieted them and said it evidently was a misunderstanding. He promised to go to Saginaw the next day and inquire about the matter. He interviewed the government agent and soon returned, bringing the good news to the worried and brave women that the stories were false.

Since Chief Bemassikeh was dead the men requested the missionary to take part in their meetings and to permit the use of the schoolroom for them. Permission was gladly given. It is remarkable how

---

[*]William Loehe, a Lutheran clergyman in Neundettelsaw, Germany, was the force behind the German Lutheran Missionary Society and training school for missionaries to be sent to foreign lands. Frankenmuth, Michigan was founded as a result of Loehe's interest in bringing the gospel to the native Americans.

well the Indians conduct their meetings. Each one speaks freely and often at great length. No one interrupts the speaker. It never happens that two or three speak at the same time. If the speech does not please them there is complete silence. They think the complete silence is more effective than a long argument.

The missionary only spoke when he was asked. He did not wish to interfere in their tribal affairs. If, however, they proposed something that was foolish, he told them plainly and showed them the consequences of their procedure. They were always willing to listen to his advice and were grateful for it.

The missionary at one time invited the men to be his guests. His home was always open to them and no day passed without a call. His sociable wife made no distinction between them and the members of her household. Whenever the missionary intended to make a long trip or returned from one, as well as on other occasions, he called all the men and women, Christian and heathen, together. Naturally the house was too small, but there was room outside. A number of long tables were set up. These tables were made of boards which were placed on flour barrels and covered with white cloth. Benches were from the school and served as chairs. Venison, corn, and clean well-water were served.

The missionary said the table prayer and then served the meat. His wife served the corn. It was passed around. No one touched anything until everyone was served. They all took notice of how the host used his knife and fork and they did likewise, without being asked. In former times the wife of the chief would put her hand into the kettle without any formalities and grab a piece of meat. Now everything had changed. Such community meals not only made the Indians use their intellect, but also gave them the eager desire to learn good manners. The Indian cannot be driven by force, but is willing to adopt good manners if he is shown in a tactful manner.

Now that the Indians included the missionary in their meetings, he also called a council meeting of which he was the presiding officer as well as the principal speaker. In late winter the Indians had to go through hard times with real hunger pangs. The hunt was poor at this time. The game had gone back into the deep forest and thicket areas. The little corn the women had raised had long been consumed. While the men were on the hunt to find any kind of game, the women literally would bend over to suppress the pangs of hunger. It was amazing how they could endure privation with intense fortitude. It pained the missionary to see their distress. Therefore he called a meeting in the schoolroom and explained the situation. How easy it would be for the men to clear more land and plant more corn. Then their families would not need to suffer hunger when the hunt was poor.

He himself had set a good example by clearing several acres in a few years. He harvested an abundant supply of corn, potatoes, and several kinds of vegetables, so that he could often help them in time of need. He explained to them that he did not want to keep them from the hunt. Otherwise they would have been suspicious and would not have listened to his proposition at all. Therefore he said that they should not give up hunting, but in the intervals between they should amuse themselves by cutting down trees, clearing the land and helping the women plant more corn. They might also be able to plant potatoes and other vegetables. He offered them seed for planting corn, potatoes, beets, carrots, squash, and so forth.

This was a new kind of council meeting. No one arose to speak for or against the suggestion. A few admitted that when the hunt was poor, there was often great suffering. The others hung their heads in silence, which they always did when they were in deep thought.

The missionary said he only suggested this plan for their welfare, and that they should think it over carefully and then do what they thought best. He dismissed the meeting and all went home.

No one had given a promise. Their feelings were that this work would be below their dignity. But in a few weeks the missionary saw the shining axes swinging in the forest. The Indians seemed to be fairly good at this work. They did leave the large trees and some were mammoth, but they chopped down all the others and gathered them into piles to be burned. This had to be done with all those beautiful trees. There were many great fires and they burned for weeks. The missionary spent many late nights with his own and other Indian boys helping to keep the fires burning. The Indians now cleared the land and raised corn, potatoes, beets, carrots, pumpkins, and so forth. The soil was good and the harvest large. The result was that he never saw any more women bent over with hunger pangs in the winter.

After this first success the missionary decided to try another one. Again he called a meeting. This time the proposition was just as important, but no pressing need was evident, at least no need which the Indians recognized. However, the missionary felt that there was a real need.

108

As long as they lived in tree-bark wigwams, which they could tear down, carry away, and erect elsewhere, they lived a nomadic life. It was only at certain times that all came together in their settlement. Most of the time, some were absent because of their hunting in the forest. Those who were closely associated with the mission house left their families in the village. Others sometimes took their families with them. So there was always a coming and going and nothing was stable.

The missionary tried to induce them to build sturdy log houses as their permanent homes. He pointed out how the women and children had to suffer from the cold winters and that even in the summer the wigwams were not a suitable home. He emphasized that a log house, even a large one, could easily be built, since they could help one another. He offered to furnish the glass for windows and all the nails for the roof to the first one that would build a log house.

There was no expression of approval. The step was too daring. They felt that it would be the beginning of giving up the free roaming life. But they did not oppose the suggestion. The missionary urged them to consider the matter carefully and act according to their own conscience.

For a long time nothing happened. Finally the widowed daughter of Chief Bemassikeh came and shyly asked, "What would one receive who built the first log house?" When she was told, "Glass for the windows and nails," she replied, "I will build one." That was a pleasant surprise. With a lot of help, within a few weeks the house was completed. It had a door, two windows, a fireplace, and chimney. The missionary furnished a bed, a table and three chairs.

When the widow and her three children moved into the new house, she had many callers. For since it had been a wonder to see the first log house in the forest, it was even a greater miracle that an Indian, especially a woman, should have built one. The callers found not only room to stand and walk around, but also light in the house when the door was closed. It was unbelievable. The smoke, too, was no longer offensive, because it did not fill the room, but peacefully went up the chimney.

The missionary met the men here and not only called their attention to the difference between a log house and a wigwam but also teased them that a woman, a widow, had more courage than the men in the first venture in this endeavor. The men would not stand for that and took steps to build houses. Reservedly they came and asked about the windows and nails. In order not to dampen their zeal for building houses it was necessary to provide windows and nails for everyone. Then their enthusiasm was great.

With new permanent homes, the lives of the Indians became more settled. They were less inclined to leave their log houses than their former wigwams. They remained hunters, but did not depend upon the hunt as much as formerly, since they harvested more every year from their fields.

The winters were no longer so unbearable, especially for the women and children, since they were protected from wind and weather. More of the families stayed home and only the men went to distant hunting grounds, and even they returned more regularly on Sundays.

The two meetings in the schoolhouse and their results proved that Indians may be civilized as well as others, if one starts in the right manner. The proper way is to plant a new attitude in their minds and souls, to bring new happiness in this life and hopes for eternal life. That this is the right way has been proved.

In some areas the government tried to civilize the Indians by building log houses, clearing the land, giving them oxen, plows, and seed, even granting them an allowance of money. This, all free. The Indians let the cleared land grow over with trees again, the log houses collapsed, the plows rusted, and they kept on living in the ways of their fathers.

What would encourage an Indian to work, when he does not know what he is living for? He sees himself equal with the deer, bear, and buffalo. They do not work, yet they live. Why should he work? They live free in the forest, and that is what he wants to do till he falls down and dies, just like the animals.

It is a miserable and pitiful thing to live without God in this world. Everything will change for those whose ears are opened and hear God's voice. Then their eyes are opened and they look over the span of life, over death, and over the grave. They see their eternal home in the Father's house of God. This is open to all that believe and gladly hear His voice and do according to His words.

Here also the words of the Lord, the Father of all mankind, are fitting: "By the sweat of your face, you shall eat bread, till you return to the ground. For out of the earth you were taken. You are dust and to dust you shall return."

The work that is accomplished here, as God has commanded, is the proper work for Christians. It makes their hearts happy and keeps life young. The work that is done for nourishment, success, wealth, honor and the like is vain. It causes heartache, early aging, irritability and closes with the song of the old preacher:

It is all vanity, entirely all vanity.[*]

One is not able to civilize the Indian by making work a pleasure, by arousing new desires, providing beautiful clothes, glass beads, fiddle-faddle, and brandy. That is the mission of the traders, the egoists, the self-righteous, and such kinds. Under their jurisdiction whole tribes disappear, as the snow in the March sunshine. Only through new birth from above comes true life to a race and the family. Without new life from God, being here is like chaff, that the wind blows away.

We have gotten ahead of our story with the building of log houses for the Indians. Now we have to turn back two or three years, to see how the little church was formed in the wilderness.

---

[*]Ecclesiastes 1:2.

CHAPTER 9

IN THE CHURCH

Come here you Christian, full of joy,
To tell the friendliness of God.
Come here and let resound
Voices of thanks to our God.
Let us to the Lord of Hosts
Sing, with happy faces.
Sing, bring in beautiful ways,
That we have been richly blessed with.

In addition to all the work in the school, forest, fields, and translating, lessons about baptism and instruction for adults had to be started. The lessons were difficult for the Indian, but were needed. It was not enough, at least the missionary thought, just to explain the way of salvation. He wanted them to memorize the chief articles of the catechism. Because they could not read them they could constantly carry them with them in their minds, like an open book, whether they be in the forest, field, wigwam or on a trip. Then in case of temptation, for Satan does not spare the newly baptized either, they would be prepared with something firm, to rebuke him.

The missionary himself had had many experiences on his many trips. There were long lonesome, sleepless nights. Sometimes it does not help to just know what is right. That only means that you have

read or have heard it. The mind needs something firm to stand upon.
For that we have the catechism, proverbs of the Bible, psalms, and
hymns. All these are true nuggets of gold for the soul. Then they can
follow the words of the Apostles, "Sing to the Lord in your hearts."
No words need to be spoken, only a soft humming of hymns, psalms
of the Bible, etc., and memory will revive one and the soul will be
refreshed. Then filled with courage and boldness a person can
undertake and suffer the most difficult tasks. When we are alone with
the Lord, He is closest to us. With Him as a companion there is no
night or darkness, no wilderness to be afraid of and no load too heavy
to carry. One of the first adults who came to the instructions was the
widowed daughter of Chief Bemassikeh. She later built the first log
house. She had a very poor memory and after days of instruction had
not been able to memorize anything. In three full days she had not
been able to memorize the first sentence of the first commandment.
The words are "Ninnindan Tebinged au Kitschimanito," "The Great
Spirit, I am the Lord your God."

She lost her patience, got very angry, left, and did not return. She
remained away for several days. When she returned, much of her
anger had disappeared and the misunderstanding was gone. She
learned slowly and with greater difficulty than some of the others. She
continued to be a true Christian and brought great happiness to our
hearts.

The old blind grandmother[*] of Pauline, who was the first one
buried in the Christian cemetery at Bethany, also came. She was the
oldest woman in the village. No one really knew the number of her
winters. She herself only knew that she was a young girl during the
American War for Independence. According to that she was in her
eighties. In spite of her old age she learned as well as the others and
was an extraordinarily good Christian. After she was baptized she
wanted to die and looked forward to that day. But it was God's will
that she had to suffer yet before that day.

She started to get severe headaches. She would squat down and
press her head on the ground while loudly whining and crying. She
would visit the missionary often. He would read the Bible stories of
Jesus suffering on the cross. At first, because of the pain she seemed

---

[*]See Appendix III, Sarah, marker number 4.

not to hear, but after a while she became more quiet. Then she would sit up and thank him for reading. She said, "The suffering of my Lord took away my suffering." This went on for many weeks. Then she said, "But before I die, I would like to be free of these pains, help me to ask God?"

The missionary did as he was asked and begged the Lord to fulfill her wish. Soon the pain was completely gone. But she did not die yet, as everyone had expected, but became very lively again. Now she did not miss a church service. Even in winter, when she lived with her family some distance from the church, she would take her cane in one hand, the other hand she laid on the shoulder of her grandson. They came up hill and down dale, three miles to church.

She would stay over noon hour at the missionary's and then attend the afternoon service. The refreshments that the wife of the missionary served her were accepted with emotional thankfulness. They left as they came, back to her wigwam. When she was visited by the missionary's wife, she was also generous, and looked around till she found a number of maple sugar turtles or some berries soaked in syrup and happily gave them to her.

Long after the missionary had left the village he heard that she still, in her usual way, led by her grandchildren, attended church services. Finally the angels came and carried her soul to Abraham's bosom.

Across the river on a steep hill lived an old man with his large family. He was an Indian from the good old stamp. For him a log house was much too modern. He lived in wigwams in summer and winter. These round structures were like a sugar loaf, open at the top, for the smoke to escape from the fire, which was in the middle of the wigwam. The deerskin-covered wigwam was decorated with embroidery and painted figures on the outside.

This old man seldom came to meetings at the house of the missionary. As the missionary made house calls to all the wigwams, he also visited this old man. He preached the gospel while the old man quietly and faithfully sat by, never opening his mouth. The missionary started to speak again and made his sermon more simple so the old Indian could understand. The old man did not move or say a word. Finally the missionary said, "You do not say a word!" "I do not want to say anything," grumbled the old man. "If I do say something, you will never stop preaching." Silence was the Indians' usual death sentence to an unfavorable sermon. The missionary said, "I did not come here to annoy you. If you prefer not to listen, I will go. But it is a good word that I brought to you. Maybe some other time you will be in a better mood to listen and accept it." Then he got up and left.

The old man was not at all hostile. He couldn't be, that would have been against the open and solemn acceptance of the missionary by the tribe, which had a far greater meaning than he ever believed at the beginning. Without this solemn acceptance, each could have handled or mishandled things in his own way. Now he commanded honor and friendship as a member of the tribe. At least they always pretended they were friendly and they always were.

The old man remained a heathen, but his grown children became Christians and brought much satisfaction to the missionary. His son was the first Indian to marry an Indian maiden in the log church. No matter how simple the Christian wedding was in the wilderness, it was the right way to start. This nice young couple was respected and remained true Christians.

Next to the home of the missionary lived a respected family. The name of the head of the family was Pemagojin Kiwdein, the North Wind. The son of his house was among the first ten to be baptized. His brave mother, a lady of great dignity and behavior, followed the children. The husband, Pemagojin, remained a hard heathen. Yet, every now and then he came into the mission house. He would sit there and smoke his peace pipe.

One time when the missionary was gone on a long trip, as it often happened, the wife and the maid were alone with the Indians. Pemagojin seemed to feel it his neighborly duty to smoke his peace pipe and be guard sitter at the same time. Naturally they could only speak a few words to each other, but that meant nothing because he was awfully quiet. Occasionally he would bring another man with him and they sat there all evening, till ten or eleven o'clock, with the two women. The women at first were filled with fear and did not know what this was all about. Then they realized that he had only good intentions and that he was a neighborly safety guard, a custom of the Indians.

When the missionary was home, Pemagojin would also come and sit quietly. To entertain him, the missionary brought out his precious Bible pictures, which he used for instructions of Bible stories with good results, for the Indians live through their eyes. They can see the game in the forest, the fish in the river, where the missionary sees nothing. So they also have a sharp eye for pictures and a good comprehension.

The missionary explained these pictures to him occasionally and he received a friendly grunt from the Indian, a sign of being pleased. But when asked if he wanted to become a Christian, he gave a short and determined, "Ka, Kamin!"—no never! It went on this way for a long time. But he would always come back and sit there for hours. If the missionary happened to be busy, he would leave as quietly as he came. The missionary noticed that lately he let his head hang more, a sign of deep thinking.

One day Pemagojin's wife came over, her face beaming with joy. She stood before the missionary and shyly looked at him. "What is it?" he asked. "Yes, my husband wants to become a Christian, but he is ashamed to tell you," she said. He answered, "There is no need to be ashamed, if there is something good ahead. I am happy that God has turned his heart. Tell him I invite him to come." She did and he came immediately.

Instructions started. The man learned as a child in his quiet, thinking way. He acquired much knowledge and insight, that now were put to good use. To instruct that kind of a heathen is a special pleasure and a blessing. Thereby many difficulties are forgotten. The missionary thought about this for a long time. The Indians had been cheated so often by the white man that they had lost all confidence in them. They were not as submissive as some heathen. They still thought of themselves as lords of the land and the white man as intruders and destroyers of their hunting reserves.

Therefore, this farsighted man found it necessary to know not only what the new stranger taught, but also his way of life. This was the reason for the many long visits. Now he had tested him for three years and watched him, so his final move was not made in haste.

When this man of the wild came to be baptized, he was like a child, tenderhearted and obedient. His entire life was changed after he became a Christian. The missionary's home was always as his father's home. Even after he had his own log house, when he planned to be away for a number of days his last stop in the village was to see the missionary. When he came back, it was his first stop, even before he saw his wife and children. After proper greetings, he went to his own log house nearby.

This old man seemed to really love the young missionary. Even after the missionary was separated from the tribe and transferred from North America to South Asia, a half a world away from him, Pemagojin wrote a letter to him that showed his love and attachment. He also assured him of his faith, which the missionary taught him, and promised to stay faithful to his end. This letter, the sainted Dr. Graul said, was a simple violet that invaded the wilderness and was scented by the rose of Christian faith. This is the letter:

> My Father!
> Heartfelt greetings to you and your family. In spirit we reach to you with our hands, accept it as if we were with you in person. I as happy that you remembered me in your letter and am especially happy that you still call the Indians your children and that you still pray for us. I beg you to always do that because I am in need of it. Further more be assured that I will, as I have promised you and my Lord at my baptism, be faithful to the end, in the faith and doctrine in which I was instructed from the beginning. I will remain unmoved till my dying day.

We will hear more about him later.

As the little Christian flock grew, the missionary had to think about introducing an organized church service and a church building. But he could not decide if he should use money from the mission budget. His own budget was not enough to build a church, yet he would gladly use all the means that he had, because the building was needed. So he decided to go ahead and pursue the plan.

It could only be a log church, as no other materials were available. The logs were free but the trees had to be cut and hewn and then erected. This again took a lot of hands, some that could wield an ax better than the missionary could.

As it was to be a church and not just another log house, his plan was to have a steeple with a cross on top of the church. A bell would be inside of the steeple. The steeple was to have eight pillars with an eight-cornered roof, topped with a round globe to represent the terrestrial globe, that is, the earth. Now, the church was designed according to his ideas, but it was not yet built.

Mission home and church

A carpenter was needed but none was available, not even in the German colony of Frankenmuth. Finally a miller's apprentice was found. He was a young man with foresight and did not want to be responsible for anything. He said, "Mr. Missionary, I can handle an ax, but that is all. If you say chop here, I will chop here, if you say chop there, I will chop there, but I cannot promise anything more." "That will be alright, I will do the thinking for you and you will do the chopping for me," answered the missionary. "Something should come out of that." So he took the miller with him from the Frankenmuth colony to his wilderness.

Here were two masters of which one knew as little as the other, each trying to accomplish something that neither had seen before. The greatest problem was the eight-cornered steeple. "Make a four-cornered steeple, Mr. Missionary, that would be much easier," said the miller. "That would be alright but it would not be as nice," was the answer. They laid it out on the even ground in front of the house, to get a clear idea of how large it had to be. After a lot of rearranging they found a plan and size that looked like a fairly good pattern. Now to make the crown or cornice that would hold the eight pillars on the bottom and top. That again took some time to figure out. But soon they had the idea. The eight pillars were no problem. After the eight-cornered roof with the globe and cross built on the top was completed the entire structure was lifted into place. This took a great deal of effort. The cross and globe were painted with white oil paint to keep them from becoming weather-beaten. The missionary had to do the painting as no one else dared to go that high. After the shingles* were cut and split he also had to nail them down on the entire roof.

This little church was attached to the end of the missionary's log house so that his study became the sacristy at the same time. The church had three high windows on each side. Just below the steeple and above the steps was the entrance to the church.

A bell was added in the steeple. It was cast in Chicago on the shores of Lake Michigan by a German man. The bell had a loud and beautiful tone. It could be heard for miles in the silent wilderness. This pleased the Indians very much.

---

*These should be referred to as shakes. They were not tapered.

In the interior of the church were to be two rows of benches, a pulpit and an altar. These required skill again. The rough board pulpit was not much to look at but a deaconess from Dresden, Germany, had sent material for an altar cloth and there was enough left over to cover the pulpit.

The old count of Einsiedel, Germany, contributed a beautiful crucifix embellished with gold figures, and a pair of candlesticks. The little church was almost completed but it had not been easy for the builder. The limited strength of the missionary was exhausted. But now he had to ride fifty miles to Saginaw to raise some money to finish the work.

As he entered the store where he always traded, the busy American asked what he needed. "This time I do not need anything, except a sum of money." "Nonsense, you know that we take in very little money," said the American. "All the same, today I need nothing but money," was the answer. "Are you serious?" he asked. The reply was "Yes." The merchant laid one hundred dollars on the table. "Will that do?" he said. "Yes, do you want a promissory note?" he asked. "Not from you," was the answer. The missionary took the money, thanked him, mounted his horse, and rode on in a happy mood. In this land where the dollar is supposed to be king, a poor missionary on his word could receive that many dollars with no promissory note.

Now he also had to think about paying back his debt. A Pastor H., whose name the missionary had never heard before, from far-off East Sea, Russia, sent him a sum of money through the mission at Leipzig for his personal use. This was the first down payment on his debt and in time other payments were made. As there was no note, the merchant would take no interest. He was friendly and even offered to give the missionary financial help whenever it was needed.

While the church was being built it was necessary to prepare a liturgy for the altar service. This again was a difficult task. The language of the Indians is very rich in the realm of visible things, but it is inadequate in the field of abstract things. They cannot describe invisible things but only things that one sees with one's eyes, such as a bear by a hunter. For example, there are eight different words for a bear. There was no knowledgeable interpreter around at the time. It required a great deal of effort to find the right expression to interpret faith. At last, however, a beautiful service was started in the church, blessed with a heavenly benediction. Every Sunday, not only all the Christians but also the unconverted assembled in the church. Also, each morning after sunrise and again every evening before sunset the church bell rang. This was not an empty prayer bell at which no one prayed, but was the call to assembly for morning and evening devotions.

Immediately after the bell rang the family and members of the household of the missionary gathered in the church, sang German hymns, heard the gospel from the German Bible and prayed in the German language. After they left, the missionary prepared for the attending Indians. They sang a hymn, read the gospel from the New Testament and said a prayer in their language. This went on for many years. It was according to the gospel of the Apostles, "Let the word of God richly live among you."

What you expect of the unchurched you must practice yourself. Indians are keen observers and their observations are incredibly accurate. If they had seen that the missionary and his household did not have a regular organized morning and evening service, they would never see why they should have regular devotions. They of course could not see the missionary on his knees in his little chamber every morning praying for help from above for the tasks ahead of him for that day. Likewise in the evening praying for faith and strength for the new life for himself. But what they could not see they sensed after awhile. Even if his face did not shine like that of Moses, they could feel from his peace and love that his soul had been newly nourished. In its own time it was made known.

Their behavior during the services now was much better than it had been in the log house. The missionary tactfully did not attempt to have perfect order. If he had pressed for perfect order many of the Indians would have stayed away. They are a proud people. But now they had an inspiring edifice and it was no longer necessary to insist on order. Because the Christians were perfectly orderly the unchurched looked to them as a model. It was obvious to them that the church was a special place where they gathered for the divine service.

Here no unchurched man thought of smoking or women of talking. It was a place respected by all people. Even though the bedroom can be a small chamber for a Christian to better communicate in private with God than in a church, yet it is different with these that have just been brought in from the wilderness to communicate with

God. At the same time there is something special in a large assembly for church services.

Even in outward appearance, the household of the missionary had a positive influence on the Indians. Formerly the Indians were not accustomed to wash themselves and they wore their clothing till they were dirty rags. Now they had a wash day. When they came to church on Sundays they were wearing clean clothes and had combed hair. So striking was the change that when the president of the mission committee, Pastor Sievers, came to visit the mission he was happily surprised. He said to the missionary, "I must confess that I have not made as much progress with some of my people as you have with the Indians." The missionary replied, "I have never spoken to them about it nor have I ever admonished them. They observed it in my house." His home was like a parent's home where all the Christian Indians were taken in and received a friendly welcome. This contributed much to regulating their habits.

Through Pastor Sievers the activities of the Indians were made known in the other German colonies. Later other visitors came. One time seven men came with Pastor Cloeter* to see the Christian Indians. Naturally this was a long trip and they were getting tired. It was nearly dark and they still could not see the end of the forest. Some said they could not go any farther and wanted to rest overnight in the forest. Suddenly, they heard the church bell ringing, loud and clear, that called the congregation to the evening blessings. That brought life into their tired limbs. They were filled with wonder to hear a church bell ringing in the forest. This filled them with energy and they arrived before dark.

There was great activity in the village when they saw so many white faces at the same time. The Indians had never seen a thing like this before. The friendly group found lodging in the log house. The next morning the church and classroom were inspected. Then, after the early morning sound of the church bell, the German service took place, hymns, prayers, etc. Then as always the Indian service followed. The steeple attracted a lot of attention. The Germans did not have steeples on the churches in their colonies yet, even though they had larger log churches.

---

*Pastor Cloeter was pastor of the Holy Cross Lutheran Church in Saginaw.

They were especially interested in the school and happy to hear the children sing hymns, even though they did not understand the Chippewa language. The German melodies made them feel at home.

After this they visited the Indian homes. Many of the Indians were scattered in the forest in temporary huts at this time of the year because it was maple sugar time. Pastor Cloeter and his friends were again surprised at the friendly reception they received at all of the homes. They felt as if they were close acquaintances.

Their faith in the Lord banished all mistrust in the Indians for the white man. Instead of mistrust, there was love and confidence. The visitors did not leave even one hut without receiving a trinket or a little figure made of maple sugar. Even the old blind Sarah would not let them leave till she pawed around in her nook and found a piece of sugar that she handed to them with a warm smile. No one dared to refuse anything.

The "Cross Tour," as the Indians referred to Pastor Cloeter and his seven visitors, returned to the log house with a bundle of maple sugar.

Pastor Grossmann came from Saginaw with a guide. He had been sent to Saginaw by Pastor Loehe. Later he went to Iowa to help the German people there form a new synod. He broke down in tears when he saw what could be accomplished among the American Indians by the word and the cross. His heart was filled with love for his Lord. After being strengthened by a German church service he returned to Saginaw and then on to the unknown, far from his home.

Things were getting more home like in Bethany. To the little one that was born in the harshest part of the winter were added two more little ones* in a warmer part of the year. One in September and the other in May. This time there was no shortage of food for the mother and child, who were confined to the bed. Help for the parents came again from above. The half-Indian midwife also came again and did what she could. She knew what to do as she was a mother herself. These wilderness babies were healthy in body and soul. For a long time, a crooked sassafras root was their only toy. They were carried around by the Indian children for walks and also in the Indian canoe. If the father arrived home from a long trip the children were not satisfied

---

*Theodosia was born December 31, 1848. Theophile was born September 28, 1950. Ullvike was born May 7, 1852.

till each had their turn at a short horseback ride. The faithful horse put up with this in spite of being tired from the journey. Often the father rode with two children in his arms. If the children were tired, they would fall asleep in his arms as he would sing or hum the tune,

> With the Lord in my heart,
> I sleep peacefully.
> I dream of paradise.
> With the Lord in my eyes,
> No enemy can scare me.
> He watches the one that prays.
> With the Lord in my thoughts,
> Bad things stay away
> Sin is avoided,
> With the help of the Lord.

In the morning the children kneeling beside their beds with folded hands prayed:

> Dear God, I pray to thee,
> A pious child you let me be.
> Should this not be
> Then better take me from this earth,
> And take me to your heavenly home
> Then make me equal with your angels.

At bedtime they did the same and repeated the prayer:

> Jesus, Thy blood and righteousness,
> Thy beauty are my glorious dress
> With Thee before my God I stand
> When I shall reach the heavenly land.

They were healthy children and no childhood diseases touched them.

It was homelike in the wilderness. The little apple and peach trees blossomed and bore their first fruit. The missionary's wife raised these from seed, then planted them in the little garden by the front door. They were seen by the one who planted them but she did not see the fruit when it ripened. Only the strawberries that she had planted in the border of her garden gave her some fruit. They had strawberries for two years but the trees bore no fruit for them. There were problems ahead that they did not know of.

CHAPTER 10

DEPARTURE

Never did the earth so happily blossom,
Never did the sun so smilingly shine,
As today it blossoms and smiles.
Now that we have to depart from here,
Part from the wigwam and log houses.
Part from the Indians we love
As only parents love their children.
Part from the little church,
And from the altar's high position.
Part from the red sons of the forest,
That bowed their knees with us.

The change in this humble place depended on circumstances, as did the entrance of our Lord at the Mount of Olives. Today it quickens the spirit when we look at it. A short time after the missionary's arrival it was named Bethany, and in a short time this Indian settlement, through the entrance of the Lord, became much different. Through comfort, planning, and hope, a new, delightful place developed.

Here and there stand a few bark wigwams, but between them stands a row of new log houses. Others are in the process of being built. The little church with the mission house is located on the highest spot. It is the source from which all activities radiate and the center to which all are drawn. The attitude of the entire village has changed.

Instead of suspicion and thoughts of murder, now love and confidence rule.

The traders who had erected a whiskey store only two miles from the settlement so they could sell whiskey to the Indians, which was illegal according to the laws of the land, did not cause any more trouble. At times the Indians were tempted to drink and that made it hard for others not to follow. The missionary had visited the two Americans who operated the store and had a friendly heart-to-heart talk with them. He begged them not to interfere with his work among the Indians. They laughed at him. When he discussed with them that it was unlawful to sell whiskey to the Indians in this area they boldly answered that they would take care of that. Then answered the missionary, "If so, then all I can do is to bring it to the Highest Court." He left depressed. Later he heard that if he had not left then they would have thrown him into the river from the high bank.

They thought that he was going to bring his complaint before the government but his reference was to the court of God because to Him no evil-doer can stand up. The help from above soon came. Only a few days later one of the men hastily gathered everything that he could lay his hands on, money and goods, and took off. The other now had nothing left. The Highest Judge punished one scoundrel with the other one. The mission was freed from this evil, as they never returned.

The place was still lonesome and was far away from any town. The trail that formerly could be seen only by a trained eye was now fairly well marked by the many trips that the missionary had made. There was room for only one horse abreast but most of the obstacles had been taken care of by the missionary's ax. He always remembered what his guide had told him: "It is important to always carry an ax in one's belt."

Travelers who came to visit the village were pleased with the beautiful arrangement. They remarked that the long lonesome trail had been cleared.

It was comfortable now. There were no fever problems here, which plagued other colonies while they were clearing the forest. The higher area and the excellent drinking water had much to do with this. The water was not from a flowing spring, but from a well that the missionary had dug. He had lined it with stones that he had gathered from the river bed. There was fresh clear water even in the hottest and driest time of the year. This was also something new for the Indians. It was here, as in the city of Nahor* in Bible days, where the women came and drew water for their camels. Even though the Indians did not have camels the women drew water for themselves and their children.

An American family decided to settle near the village. The husband was of German descent, as indicated by his name. All he knew was that his grandmother always read a large German book. He had a wife and three children. When he brought his youngest child to be baptized, the missionary found that the others had never been baptized, nor was the mother. After the children were baptized, the mother attended instructions and was then baptized. They were decent people. The husband helped with the mission work and the mother volunteered to help with the washing and sewing.

The husband also recommended that a young bride of his acquaintance, who lived a hundred miles away, come to Bethany to be treated by the missionary. She was sick and had chest problems. Her glands were swollen and she limped. The missionary did what he could and the swelling and the limping left her. The story then went out that the missionary was also a "great medicine man." The chest problem was not easily cured. She was happy that she did not limp any more and that the swelling had gone down. When her bridegroom came to visit her in the middle of the winter, she was able to go home with him.

An assistant for the missionary had arrived from Leipzig, Germany, in November 1851. His name was Ernst Miessler. He served as a teacher in the school and took many trips for the missionary. To a certain extent the loneliness and helplessness were removed. It began to be very comfortable in the wilderness.

Entirely unexpectedly a call came for the missionary to transfer from North America to southern Asia. From the cold and snow-covered wilderness he was to go to the warm, sunny palm land of India.

This was not the first call that he had received. Because of his frequent sickness and asthma the synod had recommended a milder climate and a German congregation. The missionary did not accept the recommendations. He had signed the contract that he would faithfully perform the duties of a missionary to the Indians. Above all, his call was an inner call and could not be changed in an ordinary manner. He

---

*Genesis 24:10-20.

loved the Indians too much to leave them for the comforts and ease of this life.

This call was entirely different. His original call came from the mission board in 1846. The same board had later sent him to the Indians in America. He explicitly, publicly, and solemnly had been appointed as a delegate to go to India. Only an unexpected illness had prevented him from accompanying the other four delegates to India. All this had to be seriously considered.

There was no doubt that it was his duty to follow where he was called, and this was a mission call. But there was concern about how his Indians would fare. To him it did not seem possible to leave them.

He already had been supplied with an assistant from the mission board in Leipzig. By this time the assistant was already quite familiar with the mission. He was faithful and willing to learn. He did lack experience and self-reliance and for this reason he had not been sent to India. It also seemed to not have been his gift to relate to the Indians nor to understand their point of view.

Now it was necessary to consult the mission board of the Missouri Synod, of which Bethany was a member. They agreed that the missionary should accept the call. Now there was nothing in his way, so he prepared to go to India.

So far the missionary never thought of the difficult one-thousand-mile trip and of four to six weeks on the ocean with three small children. He would have to go from New York all the way to Bremen, Germany. The missionary also forgot how seasick his wife had been when she came to America. Now the faithful maid felt that it was her duty to accompany her mistress to Germany.* With God in mind she decided to go. She had no problem with seasickness and would be able to take care of the children at sea. She would take no wages and said that she had money enough to pay her fare. Just to accompany her mistress and family was her burden in God.

Such attachment and faithfulness of a domestic servant was exceptional. She traveled with them by land and by sea, by wagon and by train. She was a priceless helper. She was the one who later told Pastor Loehe of Neundettelsaw about her experience among the Indians.

---

*Baierlein's wife was pregnant. She gave birth to a son while in Germany on her way from the United States to India.

The missionary thought it would not be good for her to go on to India as she had offered to do. So she returned to America. She was an exceptional example of a faithful maid. She did not work because of the wages, but for the will of the Lord and with love for His work. The mission family thanked her for her faithfulness with a remembrance and bestowed God's blessings on her future.

Now that as many arrangements as possible had been made to provide the Indians with the word of God, it finally was time to inform them of the impending change. A few had already foreseen what was coming.

The missionary chose for his text the one that St. Paul had preached at his farewell to the oldest church at Ephesus (Acts 20:17–35). This was a very appropriate text for this occasion.

The tension was noticeable and the Indians were waiting for the unexpected. It was announced at the end of the sermon. "Now my friends, I have loved you from the beginning and have enjoyed living among you. You accepted the word of God and that made my soul rejoice. I then loved you even more. I always thought that I would be spending the remaining days of my life in your midst. That when God called me, my bones would rest with your bones until the resurrection. I never thought of leaving. But you know that I have often told you, 'The thoughts of God are not our thoughts and His ways are not our ways.' We do not always understand His ways, but they are always good, wise and just. Now God my Lord calls me out of your midst to go far away across the ocean. The name of the place I do not even know yet. Now his servant must obey His voice and follow Him," etc.

There was much weeping among the Indians. The men with bowed heads tried to hide their feelings as is their custom. But the women, children, and the young covered their faces and wept bitterly. They were assured that they would not be forsaken and would be faithfully provided with the same true word of God in the future. At first it did not seem to sink in and they would not be consoled. For days they almost acted as if they were angry. Some said, "The Father is forsaking his children." Others groaned, "We will be all scattered."

The president of the mission board, Pastor Sievers, and his wife came the long distance to be present at the departure of the missionary and to console the Indians. He held a meeting that even the unchurched were invited to. He assured them of the continuous love and care the Missouri Synod had for them. Here again the Indians behaved as only Indians can. Some stepped forward and said what was in their hearts in a quiet but firm way. No one interrupted the other. Each one that wanted to speak rose and expressed his sorrow over the coming departure of their father and their concern for the future. Again Pastor Sievers made every effort to comfort them and to relieve all worry about their future.

At last an unchurched Indian stood up and spoke. It was Misquanoquod, the Red Cloud, the most important chief in the area. He said, "I do not belong to this congregation, but my wife and children do. I wish to say a few words. Even if we should all stand up and extend our hands to our father, in order to keep him here, he will not permit himself to remain for he is called and will go. But if we can get a man in his place, who would do as he has done, then we may still hold together. But if not, then I fear that it will be with us as a heap of dry leaves when the wind blows. *Nindike*."

These words were the last that the Indians spoke at the church meeting. This prophecy was fulfilled. Both sayings of Red Cloud came true within a few years.

During the last days the house was filled with visitors. The blind old Sarah came twice a day in spite of her frailty. Also the quiet Pemagojin came daily and sat quietly with bowed head. Every time he arose to leave he would say, "I will not see you depart. I cannot see it and do not want to see it." He would come again the next day and repeat the same words. The day before the missionary left he came and sat quietly for a long time. The missionary was busy packing, but every now and then would go over to him and put his hands on his shoulders and try to comfort him. Suddenly the old man got up, stormily embraced his beloved missionary, kissed him (something that had never happened before) and without another word, stormed out of the house and into the forest. He kept his word. He never saw the departure of the missionary. Some day in our heavenly home with God they will meet again.

The final day of departure arrived. There were many tears. The farewells to the friends and relatives when they left the homeland in Germany were not as painful as leaving this beloved place of wigwams, log houses, and forest. The Indians clung to him as though they were his own children. Early in the morning the canoes were loaded. The wife and children had already taken their places. Many Indians stepped into their own canoes to accompany them down the river. The missionary was still kneeling at the altar of his little log church praying for his red children and for strength for himself. Finally, he had to wrench himself away and leave the beloved place. One more glance at the crucifix on the altar. Now, more calm, he stepped into the empty log house once more. As he was about to leave, Pastor Sievers came toward him and said, "You cannot leave this house without receiving the thanks and appreciation of the mission board for all that you have accomplished here." The two men embraced, then hand in hand silently walked to the river.

At the river there were more silent handshakes, but the sobbing was loud. Nobody could speak. The missionary stepped into the canoe, the men pushed the canoe into the river. Pastor Sievers stood on the bank and in a loud voice began to sing:

> All Glory be to God on high,
> Who hath our race befriended
> To us no harm shall come nigh,
> The strife at last is ended.
> God showeth His good will to men
> And peace shall reign on earth again
> Oh, thank Him for his Goodness.

The missionary family joined as well as their aching hearts and faltering voices permitted. Thus they left the forest primeval!

> My home is there above
> With all the hosts of angels
> Praising their Lord and Master.
> Who entirely alone
> Has all things in His hands,
> And holds them forever and ever
> According to His pleasure.

133

A BRIEF ACCOUNT OF THE MISSION AFTER
BAIERLEIN LEFT MICHIGAN

Baierlein needed an assistant to help in the mission activities at Bethany and requested a trained helper from the German Mission Society through Pastor August Craemer of Frankenmuth.

Gustav Miessler, as he signs his name,[*] was born January 12, 1826 in Riechedbach, Goerlitz, Silesia, and died in Chicago March 1, 1916. He entered the missionary school in Leipzig, Germany, in late 1848 and graduated in 1851. He was sent to America to assist Baierlein at Bethany and arrived November 10, 1851. He became full director of the Bethany mission on May 19, 1853, after Baierlein left for India.

Miessler was given an assistant, Missionary Edmund J. Raeder, who had been assisting Missionary Auch at Sebewing, Michigan. Raeder came with his wife and a maid, who were most welcome at Bethany. After about one and one-half years Pastor Raeder left to pastor in Canada. Shortly before Raeder left, Miessler married [November 23, 1854] Johanna J. H. Pinhepant, born May 4, 1831, died July 22, 1857. She is buried with her infant son—the only white persons buried in the Bethany Indian Cemetery.[**]

Miessler was married to Caroline L. Hunning Fick, widow of Pastor W. Fick, in 1858. She was born June 7, 1833 and died July 21, 1871. On December 3, 1858 Carl Frederick Otto was born at Bethany.

The Missouri Synod Mission Society purchased a tract of land and distributed it to the Bethany Lutheran members with the under-

---

[*]His full name was Ernest Gustav Herman Miessler. His parents called him Herman, his relatives, Ernest. He signed his correspondence Gustav.

[**]See Items 8 and 9 in Appendix III.

standing that they would clear the land, build cabins, plant crops, and eventually pay for the land.

After Baierlein left, school and church services were continued sporadically. The men were increasingly absent from Bethany because the game were being displaced by over-hunting and by settlers moving into the area.

The Treaty of the United States of America with the area Indians expired in 1855 and a new treaty was negotiated. This involved giving each Indian family eighty acres of land and each single adult forty acres, in six designated townships in Isabella County. As the Bethany Indian youth had some education, they obtained jobs in the reservation administration, in logging operations, as store clerks, etc. One of the stipulations of the reservation treaty was an attempt to disband the tribal set-up and promote agriculture and industry instead of the nomadic hunting and fishing life.

Most of the Bethany Indians left and settled in two groups on the reservation. This was about seven miles north of Mt. Pleasant. Miessler followed his Bethany Indians in February 1858. Only Indians could purchase land on the reservation, so he purchased 160 acres on the west side of present Mission Avenue, where Central Michigan University is now located.

The Bethany mission site was rented to Miessler's brother-in-law, Meyer. In order to be closer to his Bethany Indians the missionary taught in one of the public schools located near his Indians. Church services were held in the members' homes. Miessler later built a combination school and church on the reservation.[*]

The crops planted by the Indians were partial failures in the years 1863–1865 because of late frost and early fall freezes. Hence the Indians were compelled to leave the reservation for hunting areas. In 1865 the church at Bethany had to be torn down to prevent its collapse. The Lutheran mission activity at the reservations had come to a near standstill, as Pastor Sievers, the mission society director, reported in 1866. The Bethany mission farm was sold to Peter Gruet, brother of the mission interpreter, James Gruet. The proceeds of the sale were used to rebuild the missionary's home in Mt. Pleasant.

---

[*]The editor believes he has located the site of the building just north of Spring Creek, three miles east of Rosebush and one-half mile south, on the east side of the present road.

Mission activity continued to decline and in 1869 the Missouri Synod advised Miessler to await a call to any church group, preferably as near the mission as possible. Not having received a call, he taught school at Holy Cross Lutheran church in Saginaw for two years, leaving in 1871. Here his fourteen-year-old daughter by his first marriage died and is buried in Holy Cross Cemetery in Saginaw.

The mission property at Mount Pleasant was sold. Missionary Miessler made several trips to Mount Pleasant to encourage the dwindling group of Bethany Indians.

Missionary and teacher Miessler entered Hahnenman Medical College in Chicago in the fall of 1871 and graduated two years later. He practiced medicine in Chicago from 1873 to 1899, and later in the central states. Dr. Miessler retired to Chicago at 86 years of age [1912] so he could be buried near his three children and his beloved third wife. He died March 1, 1916.

APPENDIX II

NAMES OF BETHANY INDIAN MEMBERS WHO WERE ENTITLED TO HOLD PROPERTY ON THE RESERVATION

From C. H. Rodd's List of 1855

George Naw We be zhick (chief)

Peter Pay Ma Se Gay

I Yalk

Elijah Ah be Taw Quot

Joseph Che Be Nay

Wah be gaw Me Skum

Isaac Petway Ge zhick

Peter non Gan Segay

Pay Me Go Gin

John O Me sgnaw aw maw Quot

James O pe Maw chi won

Jacob Maw Caw day we Quo

Peter Ne be Nah She

John O Saw be qnaw

James Caw ga aw ge win

Thos. Caw gay an Naw Quot

John Jones

Way Ne

Daniel Pay May Se Gay

Albert Petway way go nay be

Peen de Gay

Way Say Chi way

Mich Se Way

Negaw ne Gonse

Andrew Campeau

May Che Ke Go Nay

Waw Lodge

Joseph Pontiac

John Pontiac

Naway be She Quay

Ne gaw Ne ge won

William Westbrook

Waw bay gezhe go Quay

Job Pay can Naw Se Gay

Martha Rodd

Martha Ashman

James Gruett

Appendix III

The Bethany Lutheran Indian Cemetery

The Bethany Lutheran Cemetery was set apart on mission property near the church by Baierlein when Pauline,[*] the wife of Peter Naugassike, passed away. A large hand-hewn cross was planted and a wooden fence built around the area. The original markers were pine boards with carved data on them. There is a tradition that the head board markers were replaced by marble markers in 1901 by Dr. G. Miessler, when he was visiting his brother in Saginaw. The church records had been destroyed in the Chicago fire of 1871, and only incomplete data could be obtained from the weathered pine board markers.

In 1931, members of the Holy Cross Lutheran Church in Saginaw, who had been given possession of the one-half-acre cemetery plot, cleaned the area, installed a fence around the burial site, and rededicated the cemetery on October 11, 1931, in the name of the Missouri Synod Lutherans of the Saginaw Valley.

It must be noted here that in the 1931 clean-up the volunteer workers found the marble markers in a pile. They were reset in orderly fashion. Only the marker of Miessler's first wife was placed in its original position, marking her grave.

On September 19, 1948, a celebration of the centennial of the mission was held under the auspices of the Saginaw Valley Zone of the Lutheran Laymen's League.

Again, on Sunday, September 23, 1973, the Bethany Cemetery was rededicated on the occasion of the 125-year anniversary of the founding of the mission.

---

[*]See marker number 1.

141

Dedication tablet

To the Glory of the saving Power of Jesus Christ. In Memory of Craemer-Beyerlein-Miessler. Pioneer Missionaries of Michigan. Bethany Lutheran Cemetery is rededicated and this monument erected by the Lutherans of Saginaw Valley, Missouri Synod and the children of their day schools. "He that Believeth and is Baptized shall be saved" Founded 1848. 1931 rededicated.

Marker tablet

Bethany Lutheran Indian Cemetery.

Chicago Stone

8. Jesus Christ the same yesterday and today and forever. Heb.13:8. For there is none other name under heaven given among men whereby we must be saved. Acts 4:12. Whosoever believeth in Him shall receive remission of sins. Acts 10:43. As the records of the Evangelical Lutheran mission Church of the German Evangelical Lutheran synod of Missouri, Ohio and other states were destroyed by the great Chicago conflagration of AD 1871 the names of most of the children could not be ascertained. Suffice it that the word of God says, The Lord knoweth them that are His.
2 Tim. 2:19. Rejoice because your names are written in heaven. Luke 10:20. Whose names are in the *book* of life. Phil. 4:3

Grave Markers[*]

1. Pauline
wife of Peter
Naugassike
Baptized 1850
Died in Christ
21 June 1852
Rev. 14:18
Blessed are the dead which die in the Lord.

2. Shebageshiegoowe

---

[*]The wording and order of words and lines are exactly as they occur on the markers.

Woman
Oldest daughter of
Wabigonshkom
Died in Christ
26 June 1854
Acts 7:59
Lord Jesus receive my spirit.

3. Isaac
Baptized with Rebeckah
his wife 18 Sept 1852
Died in Christ Sept. 1859 1 Tim. 1:15
<u>Christ Jesus Came into the world to save sinners.</u>[*]

4. Sarah Miksiwe
Mother of the
Chippewa
Died 110 years old
in Christ
12 Apr. 1859
Gen. 49:18
I have <u>waited for thy</u>
<u>salvation, Oh Lord</u>.

5. Indian girl
Magdalina and C.H. Rodd, Trader, Sister of
Ph. Gruet
Died 1 year old
Jer. 31:3
With loving <u>kindness I</u> have drawn thee.

6. Son of Naugishig
Mark <u>10:16</u>
He that believeth and is Baptized shall be saved and he that believeth
not shall be damned.

7. Daughter of
Egrest Bedwewegonebe
Died 2 years old
Isa. 61:<u>10</u>

---

[*]The marble markers are weather worn. The underlined letters have been reconstructed.

He hath clothed me
with His garment of Salvation. He hath covered me with His robe of
righteousness.

9. Heir ruhet in Gott
Johanna J. H.
geborn Pinhepant
Ehe Fraw des Rev.
E.G.H. Meissler
Geboren den 4 Mai
1831
Gest den 26 Juli
1857
Ereede duer Asche
on Job 14:13.

10. J.J.H.M.*

11. Girl of J. Gruet
Still born
Luke 19:10
The Son of man is come
to seek and save that
which was lost

12. Indian Child
1 John 1:7
The blood of Jesus Christ his
Son cleanseth us from all sin.

13. Indian Child
Rom. 14:8
Whether we live therefore or die, we are the Lord's.

14. Indian Child
Is. 54:10
My kindness shall not
depart from thee

15. Indian Child
Matt. 1:21

---

*Footstone.

144

For he shall save his
people from their sins

16. Florence
Daughter of P. Gruet
Baptized
Mar[k] 10:14
Suffer the little children to come unto me and forbid them not for such
is the kingdom of God.

17. Fredrick
Son of P. Gruet
Rom. 6:23
The wages of sin is death but the gift of God is eternal life in Jesus
Christ our Lord.

18. Indian Child
Is. 57:2
He shall enter into peace. They shall rest in their beds each one walk-
ing in his unrighteousness

19. Indian Child
John 14:19
Because I live
ye shall
also love

20. Indian Child
2 Tim.5:21
For he hath made him to be sin for us, who knew no sin that we might
be made the Righteous of God in Him.

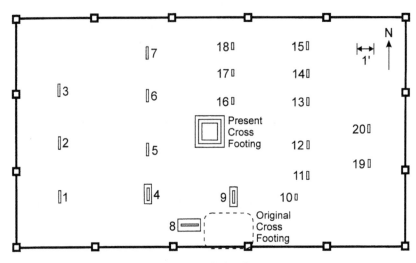

Bethany Indian Mission Cemetery

Cemetery Markers

APPENDIX IV
ORIGINAL LAND PURCHASES NEAR
THE BETHANY MISSION SITE

1. August 13, 1839. Gratiot County Tract Book. U.S.Government, to Pay me sa kee, 147.2 acres. SE 1/4 NW 1/4 40 acres, NW 1/4 NW 1/4 37.7 acres, W 1/2 SW 1/4, S18 T12N R2W.

2. October 10, 1842. Liber 4 p. 498, Gratiot County. U.S.Government, to Pay me se kee, Ah bet o quot and Pay me te ha wance quay, 240 acres. NE1/4 & W1/2 SE1/4 S18 T12N R2W

3. March 1850. Liber 4, p. 554, Gratiot County. U.S. Government to August Craemer, 40 acres. NW 1/4 NW 1/4 S18 T12N R2W.
a. Site of Bethany Lutheran Indian Mission.

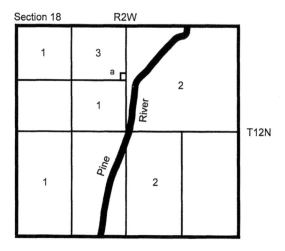

Contemporary Michigan Poetry: Poems from the Third Coast, edited by
Michael Delp, Conrad Hilberry, and Herbert Scott, 1988

Over the Graves of Horses, by Michael Delp, 1988

Wolf in Sheep's Clothing: The Search for a Child Killer, by Tommy
McIntyre, 1988

Copper-Toed Boots, by Marguerite de Angeli, 1989 (reprint)

Detroit Images: Photographs of the Renaissance City, edited by John
J. Bukowczyk and Douglas Aikenhead, with Peter Slavcheff,
1989

Hangdog Reef: Poems Sailing the Great Lakes, by Stephen Tudor, 1989

Detroit: City of Race and Class Violence, revised edition, by
B. J. Widick, 1989

Deep Woods Frontier: A History of Logging in Northern Michigan, by
Theodore J. Karamanski, 1989

Orvie, The Dictator of Dearborn, by David L. Good, 1989

Seasons of Grace: A History of the Catholic Archdiocese of Detroit, by
Leslie Woodcock Tentler, 1990

The Pottery of John Foster: Form and Meaning, by Gordon and
Elizabeth Orear, 1990

*The Diary of Bishop Frederic Baraga: First Bishop of Marquette,
Michigan*, edited by Regis M. Walling and Rev. N. Daniel
Rupp, 1990

Walnut Pickles and Watermelon Cake: A Century of Michigan Cooking,
by Larry B. Massie and Priscilla Massie, 1990

The Making of Michigan, 1820–1860: A Pioneer Anthology, edited by
Justin L. Kestenbaum, 1990

*America's Favorite Homes: A Guide to Popular Early Twentieth-Century
Homes*, by Robert Schweitzer and Michael W. R. Davis, 1990

Beyond the Model T: The Other Ventures of Henry Ford, by Ford
R. Bryan, 1990

Life after the Line, by Josie Kearns, 1990

*Michigan Lumbertowns: Lumbermen and Laborers in Saginaw, Bay
City, and Muskegon, 1870–1905*, by Jeremy W. Kilar, 1990

Detroit Kids Catalog: The Hometown Tourist, by Ellyce Field, 1990

Waiting for the News, by Leo Litwak, 1990 (reprint)

Detroit Perspectives, edited by Wilma Wood Henrickson, 1991

Life on the Great Lakes: A Wheelsman's Story, by Fred W. Dutton, edited by William Donohue Ellis, 1991

Copper Country Journal: The Diary of Schoolmaster Henry Hobart, 1863–1864, by Henry Hobart, edited by Philip P. Mason, 1991

John Jacob Astor: Business and Finance in the Early Republic, by John Denis Haeger, 1991

Survival and Regeneration: Detroit's American Indian Community, by Edmund J. Danziger, Jr., 1991

Steamboats and Sailors of the Great Lakes, by Mark L. Thompson, 1991

Cobb Would Have Caught It: The Golden Years of Baseball in Detroit, by Richard Bak, 1991

Michigan in Literature, by Clarence Andrews, 1992

Under the Influence of Water: Poems, Essays, and Stories, by Michael Delp, 1992

The Country Kitchen, by Della T. Lutes, 1992 (reprint)

The Making of a Mining District: Keweenaw Native Copper 1500–1870, by David J. Krause, 1992

Kids Catalog of Michigan Adventures, by Ellyce Field, 1993

Henry's Lieutenants, by Ford R. Bryan, 1993

Historic Highway Bridges of Michigan, by Charles K. Hyde, 1993

Lake Erie and Lake St. Clair Handbook, by Stanley J. Bolsenga and Charles E. Herndendorf, 1993

Queen of the Lakes, by Mark Thompson, 1994

Iron Fleet: The Great Lakes in World War II, by George J. Joachim, 1994

Turkey Stearnes and the Detroit Stars: The Negro Leagues in Detroit, 1919–1933, by Richard Bak, 1994

Pontiac and the Indian Uprising, by Howard H. Peckham, 1994 (reprint)

Charting the Inland Seas: A History of the U.S. Lake Survey, by Arthur M. Woodford, 1994 (reprint)

Ojibwa Narratives of Charles and Charlotte Kawbawgam and Jacques LePique, 1893–1895. Recorded with Notes by Homer H. Kidder, edited by Arthur P. Bourgeois, 1994, co-published with the Marquette County Historical Society

Strangers and Sojourners: A History of Michigan's Keweenaw Peninsula, by Arthur W. Thurner, 1994

Win Some, Lose Some: G. Mennen Williams and the New Democrats, by Helen Washburn Berthelot, 1995

Sarkis, by Gordon and Elizabeth Orear, 1995

Kids Catalog of Michigan Adventures, second edition, by Ellyce Field, 1995

The Northern Lights: Lighthouses of the Upper Great Lakes, by Charles K. Hyde, 1995 (reprint)

Rumrunning and the Roaring Twenties: Prohibition on the Michigan-Ontario Waterway, by Philip P. Mason, 1995

In the Wilderness with the Red Indians, by E. R. Baierlein, translated by Anita Z. Boldt, edited by Harold W. Moll, 1996

.